MW00890766

Complete Spanish for Middle & High School Students

3 Workbooks in 1

Learn Spanish Vocabulary, Grammar, and More! (For Homeschool or Classroom)

Book 1: Spanish Fundamentals
Book 2: Spanish words & phrases
Book 3: Spanish short stories

Table of Contents

~~$100+~~ FREE BONUSES

100 Complete Spanish Flashcards

30-Day Spanish Study Plan

100 Spanish Audio Pronunciations

Scan QR code to claim your bonuses

— OR —

visit bit.ly/48ZCcUQ

Book 1
Complete Spanish for Middle & High School Students

Spanish Fundamentals

Introduction

Why Learn Spanish?

Alright, let's start with some interesting information. Did you know...?

- There are over 40 million native Spanish speakers in the United States.
- All around the world, more than 470 million people speak Spanish as their first language. It is the second most widely spoken language globally in terms of native speakers!
- Plus, more than 20 million people are learning Spanish as their second language!

Spanish is super useful, not just because of these numbers, but also for other reasons. You might want to connect with family or friends who don't speak English, volunteer in your community, or get ready for future job opportunities. This book will guide you through the basics of Spanish in a fun and simple way.

How to Use This Book

So, how can you use this book?

- If you're learning on your own, you can follow this book along with other resources.
- If you need to look up something specific, use this book as a reference.
- If you're in a class or have a Spanish tutor, this book can be a great supplement to your lessons.

Now, let's dive into the fun part — our first lesson!

Chapter 0: ¡Ra, ra, ra!

Hablar poco, pero mal, ya es mucho hablar.
- Alejandro Casona

The Spanish Alphabet

A	a *auto* arm	B	be *banana* banana	C	ce *casa, cielo* cat, soon
D	de *dado* dog	E	e *eco* elephant	F	efe *fuego* fire
G	ge *gato, gen* go, hello	H	hache *hola* silent letter	I	i *isla* see
J	jota *jugo* heart	K	ka *kilo* key	L	ele *lunes* land
M	eme *mamá* mine	N	ene *noche* note	Ñ	eñe *ñoño, niño* Kanye
O	o *oso* Omaha	P	pe *papá* Spain	Q	qu *queso* cat
R	erre *rosa* arte	S	ese *sopa* spoon	T	te *tomate* Toronto
U	u *uva* soon	V	uve *vaca* baby	W	doble uve *wi-fi* wi-fi
X	equis *xilofón* soon	Y	y griega *yema* *soy* she see	Z	zeta *zorro* so theory

💬 G Sounds

G + A, O, U sounds like the G in "go" or "gate"
* ga (*gato*)
* go (*gota*)
* gu (*guante*)

But...
G + E, I sounds like the H in "hello"
* ge (*gen*)
* gi (*girasol*)

So, if we want the G to make a soft sound when it's before an E or an I, we need to add a silent U, as in...
* gue (*guerra*)
* gui (*guitarra*)

And, if we want the U to stop being silent, we need to turn it into an Ü, as in...
* güe (*vergüenza*)
* güi (*pingüino*)

💬 C Sounds

Before A, O, U and consonants, C sounds like a K:
* ca (*casa*)
* co (*cono*)
* cu (*cuarto*)
* cr (*cráneo*)

But...
C sounds like S when it's before an E or an I:
* ce (*celeste*)
* ci (*cielo*)

If we want to spell a word with the sounds KE or KI in Spanish, we use the letter Q and a silent U:
* que (*queso*)
* qui (*quilo*)

Remember!
Q goes always before U!

💬 R Sounds

When R appears at the start of a word or when two Rs are together, it adopts the sound of the strong Spanish R, produced by rolling the Rs, closely resembling the way "rage" is pronounced, but with more intensity. However, if it's a single R within a word, it's pronounced softly, similar to the Ts in the American pronunciation of "butter."

💬 Other sounds

- ll (*lluvia*) as in **sh**e
- ch (*chino*) as in **Ch**inese

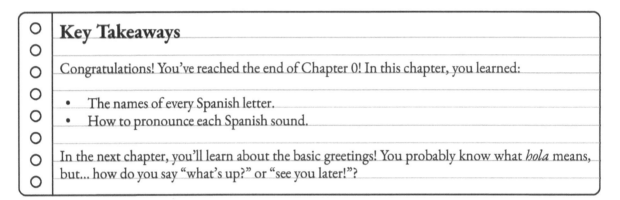

Key Takeaways

Congratulations! You've reached the end of Chapter 0! In this chapter, you learned:

- The names of every Spanish letter.
- How to pronounce each Spanish sound.

In the next chapter, you'll learn about the basic greetings! You probably know what *hola* means, but... how do you say "what's up?" or "see you later!"?

Chapter 1: *¿Qué onda?*

Si no te conozco, no he vivido.
- Luis Cernuda

Greetings and Basic Phrases

Imagine saying *Hola!* for the first time in a Spanish speaking country — exciting, right? In this lesson, you will learn the essentials of Spanish greetings. You will learn how to say hi, how to use polite words, and how to apologize.

Greet the greetings!

- *Hola*: This is a common greeting in Spanish, equivalent to saying "hello" in English. You use it to initiate a conversation or to greet someone when you meet them.
- *Buenos días*: Literally translates to "good morning." It's used as a formal greeting in the morning until around midday.
- *Buenas tardes*: It translates to "good afternoon." You can use this formal greeting from midday until the early evening.
- *Buenas noches*: This greeting translates to "good evening" or "good night." It's used to greet someone in the evening or before they go to bed.
- *Chau / Chao*: This is an informal way of saying "bye" or "goodbye" in Spanish. It's commonly used among friends and in casual settings.
- *Nos vemos / Hasta luego*: These phrases both mean "see you later." They're used to express the intention to meet again in the future, typically in a more casual setting.
- *¿Cómo estás? / ¿Qué tal? / ¿Cómo te va?*: These are all different ways of asking "How are you?" in Spanish. They can be used interchangeably in casual conversations to inquire about someone's well-being.
- *¿Cómo le va?*: This is a more formal version of the same question, used when addressing someone to whom you want to show more respect or distance.
- *¿Qué onda?*: This is a colloquial expression in Spanish, primarily used in Mexico and some other Latin American countries. It translates to "What's up?" or "What's going on?" in English. It's a very informal way to inquire about someone's current situation or to start a conversation.
- *Disculpe*: This means "excuse me" or "I'm sorry" and is used to get someone's attention or to apologize. It's a polite way to ask for assistance or to acknowledge a mistake.
- *Permiso*: This also translates to "excuse me." It's used when you need to ask for permission to do something or when you need to politely pass through a group of people.

Remember that the way you use these words and phrases can vary based on the context and the level of formality in your conversation.

💬 Possible Answers to "How are you?"

- *Bien, gracias*: "I'm well, thank you." This is a positive response, indicating that you're feeling well. You are also expressing gratitude for the inquiry.
- *Bien. ¿Y tú?*: "I'm well, how about you?" This is also a positive response and you also inquire about the other person's well being.
- *Muy bien*: "Very well." Similar to the first response, this indicates that you're feeling very good.
- *Más o menos*: "So-so." This is a way to express that you're feeling neither great nor terrible, just somewhere in between.
- *Mal*: "Bad." This is a straightforward answer indicating that you're not feeling well. You should only use this answer with close friends and relatives.

Remember that these responses can be used to convey your emotional and physical state when someone asks you *¿Cómo estás?* The choice of response depends on how you're feeling at that moment.

💬 Other Essential Words and Phrases

- *Gracias*: "Thank you."
- *De nada*: "You're welcome."
- *Por favor*: "Please."
- *Perdón / Lo siento*: "I'm sorry" or "I apologize."
- *¿Dónde queda...?*: "Where can I find...?"
  For example, *¿Dónde queda la biblioteca?* means "Where can I find the library?"

Practice Time!

Read the following text:

> *En el vestíbulo del cine, Mónica espera a su amiga Lucía. Lucía todavía no aparece, aunque la película está a punto de comenzar.*
>
> *Resignada, Mónica decide entrar sin esperar más. Se acerca a un hombre y pregunta:*
>
> *—Disculpe, buenas noches... ¿Sabe dónde está la sala número 11?*
>
> *—Al fondo a la derecha —contesta el hombre, señalando.*
>
> *Mónica agradece y avanza hacia la sala.*
>
> *Dentro, encuentra a Lucía en su asiento. Tiene un vaso de Pepsi y un balde de palomitas en la mano.*
>
> *—¡Lucía! —exclama Mónica, asombrada—. Hola...*
>
> *—¿Qué tal? —saluda su supuesta amiga.*

—*¿Por qué no respondiste mis mensajes?*

—*¡Shh! —contesta Lucía, absorta en los avances, que claramente ocupan su atención más que la charla.*

Resignada, Mónica decide sentarse a disfrutar de la película.

Translation

Now, read the translation:

In the cinema lobby, Mónica waits for her friend Lucía. Lucía still hasn't shown up even though the movie is about to start.

Resigned, Mónica decides to enter without waiting any longer. She approaches a man and asks:

"Excuse me, good evening... Do you know where auditorium number 11 is?"

"At the back, to the right," the man replies, pointing to it.

Mónica thanks him and heads towards the theater.

Inside, she finds Lucía in her seat. She's holding a cup of Pepsi and a bucket of popcorn.

"Lucía!" Mónica exclaims, surprised. "Hey..."

"How's it going?" her so-called friend greets her.

"Why didn't you reply to my messages?"

"Shh!" Lucía replies, absorbed in the previews, which clearly interest her more than the conversation.

Resigned, Mónica decides to sit down to enjoy the movie.

Practice!

Look at the short story for a minute. Then, fill out the blanks with the missing words.

En el vestíbulo del cine, Mónica espera a su amiga Lucía. Lucía todavía no aparece, aunque la película está a punto de comenzar.

Resignada, Mónica decide entrar sin esperar más. Se acerca a un hombre y pregunta:

—_____, _____ ... *¿Sabe dónde está la sala número 11?*

—*Al fondo a la derecha —contesta el hombre, señalando.*

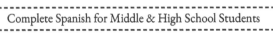
Mónica agradece y avanza hacia la sala.

Dentro, encuentra a Lucía en su asiento. Tiene un vaso de Pepsi y un balde de palomitas en mano.

—¡Lucía! —exclama Mónica, asombrada—. _____ ...

—¿_____ ? —saluda su supuesta amiga.

—¿Por qué no respondiste mis mensajes?

—¡Shh! —contesta Lucía, absorta en los avances, que claramente ocupan su atención más que la charla.

Resignada, Mónica decide sentarse a disfrutar de la película.

Go back to the original text to check your answers.

Key Takeaways

Congratulations! You've reached the end of Chapter 1! In this first chapter, you learned:

- Many phrases to greet people in Spanish, such as:
  hola, buenos días, and *buenas tardes.*
- How to ask about someone's well-being with
  ¿cómo estás?, ¿qué tal?, and *¿cómo te va?*
- How to answer with
  muy bien, bien, and *más o menos.*
- How to say goodbye in Spanish with phrases like:
  chao, chau, and *nos vemos.*
- Other basic Spanish phrases, such as:
  disculpe, por favor, permiso, and *de nada.*

In the next chapter, we'll talk about two types of words: articles and adjectives. Besides, we'll learn that every noun in Spanish has a gender. That's right! In Spanish, forks are feminine and knives are masculine!

Chapter 2: Is friendship female? Is love male?

Es tan corto el amor y tan largo el olvido.
- Pablo Neruda

Grammatical Gender

Imagine that every word in Spanish is like a character in a story and, just like in a story, each word has its own personality. Now, some words are like boys, and some are like girls. We call this "grammatical gender."

Perhaps this makes sense to you if we are talking about living beings, like a male cat (*gato*) and a female cat (*gata*). It's very reasonable to assume that *gato* is a masculine word and gata is a feminine word.

However, what if we are talking about inanimate objects or abstract concepts? It may seem strange to you, but, in Spanish, those words are gendered too!

For example, *amor* ("love") is a masculine word, and so it's *olvido* ("forgetting"), both present in this chapter's initial quote. *Amistad* ("friendship"), on the other hand, is a feminine word. This doesn't mean that Spanish-speakers see love as a male concept and friendship as a female concept. Grammatical gender doesn't have a meaning outside of grammar!

Another example: *planeta* (planet) is a feminine word, and *cielo* (sky) is a masculine word. However, bear in mind that this doesn't mean that Spanish-speakers believe that all planets are female, or that the sky is male!

Besides, Spanish is not the only language that does this. French, Italian, German and many others do the same.

Now, let's check some examples of masculine words:
*   *Perro* ("dog")
*   *Maquillaje* ("makeup")
*   *Amigo* ("male friend")

And, now, let's see some examples of feminine words:
*   *Casa* ("house")
*   *Ciencia* ("science")
*   *Amiga* ("female friend")

Learning about grammatical gender is like getting to know the characters in a story, and soon, you'll be able to tell whether each word is masculine or feminine.

Articles

Do you know what an article is? Think of them as word-helpers. They are the type of word that comes before a noun in order to let us know which thing we are talking about. Let's see an example:

• *Un pato* ("a duck")

The word *un* is the article and *pato* is the noun.

In Spanish, like in English, there are definite and indefinite articles.

The **definite articles** are:

• *El* is like saying "the" before singular masculine words. For example, *el libro* ("the book").
• *La* is like saying "the" before singular feminine words. For example, *la puerta* ("the door").
• *Los* is like saying "the" before plural masculine words. For example, *los libros* ("the books").
• *Las* is like saying "the" before plural feminine words. For example, *las puertas* ("the doors").

The **indefinite articles** are:

• *Un* is like saying "a" or "an" before singular masculine words. For example, *un libro* ("a book").
• *Una* is like saying "a" or "an" before singular feminine words. For example, *una puerta* ("the door").
• *Unos* is like saying "some" before plural masculine words. For example, *unos libros* ("some books").
• *Unas* is like saying "some" before plural feminine words. For example, *unas flores* ("some flowers").

Practice Time!

Read the following text:

> *Julieta compra comida para una fiesta. Primero, compra unos aguacates, unas cebollas, un tomate y un limón para hacer guacamole. Además, añade unos nachos y una botella de refresco.*
> *Ya en su casa, Julieta pela los aguacates, corta las cebollas, rebana el tomate y exprime el limón para el guacamole. Finalmente, sirve el refresco para sus amigos.*
> *A las diez de la noche, sus amigos llegan muy contentos. Sin embargo, al abrir la puerta, Julieta se da cuenta de que sus amigos también traen comida... nachos con guacamole.*

Ⓐ Translation

Now, read the translation:

> Julieta buys food for a party. First, she buys some avocados, some onions, a tomato, and a lemon to make guacamole. Besides, she adds some nachos and a bottle of soda.
> Back at her house, Julieta peels the avocados, cuts the onions, slices the tomato, and squeezes the lemon for the guacamole. Finally, she serves the soda to her friends.
> At ten o'clock at night, her friends arrive very happily. However, when she opens the door, Julieta

realizes that her friends are also bringing food... nachos with guacamole.

 Practice!

Look at the short story for a minute. Then, fill out with the missing words.

Julieta compra comida para una fiesta. Primero, compra _____ aguacates, _____ limón para hacer guacamole. Además, añade _____ nachos y _____ botella de refresco.

Ya en su casa, Julieta pela _____ aguacates, corta _____ cebollas, rebana _____ tomate y exprime _____ limón para el guacamole. Finalmente, sirve _____ refresco para sus amigos.

A las diez de la noche, sus amigos llegan muy contentos. Sin embargo, al abrir la puerta, Julieta se da cuenta de que sus amigos también traen comida... nachos con guacamole.

Adjectives

So what's an adjective? They are a type of word, just as nouns and articles. They are used in language to provide more information about a noun. Adjectives are used to describe or modify nouns by adding details that help give a clearer and more vivid picture of what the noun is like. They serve to give qualities, characteristics, attributes, or other descriptive elements to the noun they accompany.

For example, we can say *el perro* ("the dog"), *el perro blanco* ("the white dog") or *el perro adorable* ("the adorable dog"). *Blanco* and *adorable* are adjectives and they tell us a bit more about the dog. Also, in Spanish, adjectives usually go after the noun, not before, like in English.

In Spanish, adjectives must agree in gender and number with the nouns they modify. This means that, if a noun is masculine, the adjective that describes it must also be masculine, and, if the noun is feminine, the adjective must be feminine as well.

For example, we can say *el gato blanco* ("the white male cat") or *la gata blanca* ("the white female cat"). However, some adjectives are neutral. For example, we can say *un chico inteligente* ("a smart boy") or *una chica inteligente* ("a smart girl"). The word *inteligente* ("smart") is a neutral adjective and it doesn't change according to gender.

It is important to notice that adjectives must agree in both gender and number with the noun they modify. That means that, if the noun is plural, the adjective must be plural too.

For example, we can say *el gato blanco* ("the white male cat") or *los gatos blancos*, which can mean "the white cats" (they are not all female, at least one of them is male) or "the white male cats." If we want to say "the white female cats," we say *las gatas blancas*. This phenomenon is called the "generic masculine." To talk about a group of men and women, for example, we use the masculine.

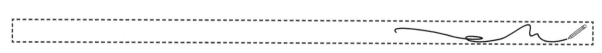

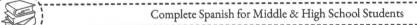

Now, how do we make the plural in Spanish? It is actually very simple: if the word ends in a vowel, we add an "s;" if the word ends in a consonant (except for z!), we add "es;" if the word ends in a "z," we erase the "z" and add "ces."

Let's check how we turn the following singular nouns into plural nouns...

*El **perro*** ("the dog") → *Los **perros*** ("the dogs")
*El **árbol*** ("the tree") → *Los **árboles*** ("the trees")
*La **luz*** ("the light") → *Las **luces*** ("the lights")

And we can also turn the following singular adjectives into plural adjectives...

*El perro **grande*** ("the big dog") → *Los perros **grandes*** ("the big dogs")
*El árbol **alemán*** ("the German tree") → *Los árboles **alemanes*** ("the German trees")
*La luz **brillante*** ("the bright light") → *Las luces **brillantes*** ("the bright lights")

Practice Time!

Read the following text:

> *Martín tiene un perro, Polo, y una gata, Violeta. Martín los quiere mucho a los dos.*
> *Polo es grande, peludo y amistoso. Violeta, en cambio, es pequeña, gris y tímida. Aunque son muy diferentes, Polo y Violeta son amigos. Durante el día, juegan juntos y, por las noches, duermen juntos en la cama de Martín.*
> *La hermana de Martín, Josefina, tiene una coneja llamada Celeste. Celeste es negra, pequeña y glotona. A veces, Violeta y Celeste duermen juntas en la cama de Josefina, pero a Polo no le gusta eso.*
> *Martín es muy responsable e inteligente, así que cuida muy bien de Violeta y Polo. Josefina adora a los animales, así que también cuida muy bien de Celeste. Por eso, todas las mascotas de la casa están sanas, felices y cómodas.*

(A) Translation

Now, read the translation:

> Martín has a male dog, Polo, and a female cat, Violeta. Martín loves them both very much. Polo is big, furry, and friendly. Violeta, on the other hand, is small, gray, and shy. Although they are very different, Polo and Violeta are friends. During the day, they play together, and at night, they sleep together on Martín's bed.
> Martín's sister, Josefina, has a female rabbit named Celeste. Celeste is black, small, and greedy. Sometimes, Violeta and Celeste sleep together on Josefina's bed, but Polo doesn't like that.
> Martín is very responsible and smart, so he takes very good care of Violeta and Polo. Josefina loves animals, so she also takes very good care of Celeste. That's why all the pets in the house are healthy, happy, and comfortable.

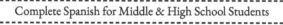
 Practice

Look at the text for a minute. Then, fill out with the missing words.

Martín tiene un perro, Polo, y una gata, Violeta. Martín los quiere mucho a los dos.

Polo es _____, _____ y _____. Violeta, en cambio, es _____, _____ y _____. Aunque son muy diferentes, Polo y Violeta son amigos. Durante el día, juegan _____ y, por las noches, duermen _____ en la cama de Martín.

La hermana de Martín, Josefina, tiene una coneja llamada Celeste. Celeste es _____, _____ y _____. A veces, Violeta y Celeste duermen _____ en la cama de Josefina, pero a Polo no le gusta eso.

Martín es muy _____ e _____, así que cuida muy bien de Violeta y Polo. Josefina adora a los animales, así que también cuida muy bien de Celeste. Por eso, todos los animales de la casa están _____, _____ y _____.

Notice that, even if Violeta and Celeste are female, the word animal is a masculine noun in Spanish. Therefore, we use masculine adjectives in the last paragraph (sanos, felices and cómodos).

Key Takeaways

Good job! That's the end of Chapter 2! In this chapter:

- We talked about grammatical gender in Spanish and we learned about feminine and masculine words.
- We introduced the Spanish articles:
  Definite articles el, la, los, and las.
  Indefinites articles un, una, unos, and unas.
- We learned about adjectives:
  They modify the noun.
  They have to agree in gender and number with the noun.
  Some adjectives, like inteligente, are neutral.
- Finally, we saw how to transform singular nouns and adjectives into the plural.

Chapter 3 is filled with knowledge! You'll learn all there is to know about the most common Spanish prepositions, so don't miss it!

Chapter 3: *¡Vamos a aprender!*

Aprender a leer es lo más importante que me ha pasado en la vida.
- Mario Vargas Llosa

Spanish prepositions

A preposition is a word that shows the relationship between a noun or pronoun and other words in a sentence. It indicates location, direction, time, manner, and other relationships.

Now, prepositions don't like to be the stars of the show. They're like the unsung sidekicks, quietly making sentences tick. Also, they are very constant, which means they don't change their shape or sound, no matter what company they keep. If they're hanging out with nouns, verbs, or other words, they stay exactly the same.

However, as every complex character, these sidekicks can be tricksters sometimes! Why? Because their usage can vary between Spanish and English. That is why it's important to practice and familiarize yourself with their usage in context to become more comfortable around them.

So, next time you're building a sentence, look for these little prepositions! They'll help you navigate the world of Spanish meanings!

Now, we'll take a look at the most common prepositions in Spanish and their uses.

💬 *A:*

- Direction or destination: *Voy **a** la tienda* ("I'm going to the store").
- Recipient: *Regalé un libro **a** mi amigo* ("I gave a book to my friend").
- Time: *Salimos **a** las cinco* ("We're leaving at five").

💬 *Con:*

- Company or accompaniment: *Salí **con** mis amigos* ("I went out with my friends").
- Means or tool: *Escribo **con** un lápiz* ("I write with a pencil").
- Manner: *Hablo **con** entusiasmo* ("I speak with enthusiasm").

💬 *De:*

- Possession: *El libro **de** María* ("María's book").
- Author: *Un libro **de** Borges* ("A book by Borges").
- Relationship: *La madre **de** Felipe* ("Felipe's mother").
- Origin or source: *Vengo **de** España* ("I come from Spain").

- Material: *Una mesa **de** madera* ("A table made of wood").
- Topic: *Una novela **de** misterio* ("A mystery novel").

💬 *Por:*

- Reason or motive: *Viajo **por** placer* ("I travel for pleasure").
- Duration: *Trabajé por **dos** horas* ("I worked for two hours").
- Exchange: *Cambio dólares **por** pesos* ("I exchange dollars for pesos").
- Medium of communication: ***Puedes contactarla por Instagram*** ("You can contact her via Instagram").

💬 *Para:*

- Purpose or goal: *Estudiamos **para** aprender* ("We study to learn").
- Destination: *El autobús parte **para** Chicago* ("The bus departs for Chicago").
- Recipient: *El regalo es **para** ti* ("The gift is for you").
- Deadline: *Necesito esto **para** mañana* ("I need this by tomorrow").

💬 *En:*

- Location: *Estoy **en** casa* ("I'm at home").
- Time: Celebramos *Navidad **en** diciembre* ("We celebrate Christmas in December").
- Manner or means: *Trabaja **en** silencio* ("She works in silence").

Practice Time!

Read the following story:

Es tarde y Matías, recostado en su cama, mira una película de terror en Netflix. Al mismo tiempo, está hablando por Whatsapp con su amiga Luciana, que, desde su casa, mira la misma película.

Matías está solo en el departamento esta noche. Sus padres han salido a una cena con amigos. El adolescente está muy feliz por tener el hogar solo para él y se está divirtiendo mucho gracias a la película y a la conversación con Luciana.

De pronto, en medio de una escena muy tensa, su amiga le envía un mensaje:

"Necesitamos hacer una pausa".

Matías, confundido, responde con otro mensaje:

"¿Por qué?".

El mensaje de Luciana no tarda en llegar:

"Oigo un ruido extraño abajo. Creo que Toto se cayó. Espera mientras voy a la sala para ver si está bien".

Matías resopla y pausa la película. Toto es el perro de Luciana. Ya está muy viejo y no ve bien. Por eso a veces se tropieza con las cosas.

Los minutos pasan y Luciana no regresa. Matías no aguanta los deseos de seguir viendo la película, de modo que vuelve a escribirle a su amiga:

"¿Holaaa?".

Luego de unos segundos, recibe una respuesta:

"Hola".

Matías se pone a escribir:

"¿Toto está bien?".

El siguiente mensaje de Luciana lo obliga a fruncir el ceño:

"No era Toto".

Confundido, Matías se incorpora en la cama, pero, antes de que pueda tipear una respuesta, ve otro mensaje:
"Y no soy Luciana".

Alarmado ya, Matías se queda en silencio por un momento. Sabe que esa noche su amiga también está sola en su casa. ¿Acaso le está jugando una broma?

Sí: debe ser eso. El adolescente responde con otro mensaje:

"Ja, ja, muy graciosa".

Distraído mientras espera la respuesta de Luciana, Matías no escucha los pasos en el pasillo hasta que suenan literalmente detrás de su puerta. Sobresaltado, se levanta de la cama al tiempo que la puerta se abre:

—¡Hola, cariño! —lo saluda su madre—. ¿Cómo estuvo tu noche?

Matías respira aliviado y se siente un verdadero ingenuo. Unos minutos después, luego de marcharse su madre, el adolescente vuelve a mirar el celular. Luciana contestó:

"Pensé que lograría asustarte. ¿Seguimos con la película?".

Ⓐ Translation

Now, read the translation:

It is late, and Matías, lying on his bed, is watching a horror movie on Netflix. At the same time, he is chatting on WhatsApp with his friend Luciana, who is watching the same movie at her home.
Matías is alone in the apartment tonight. His parents have gone out to dinner with friends. The teenager is thrilled to have the place all to himself and is having a lot of fun thanks to the movie and the conversation with Luciana.

Suddenly, in the middle of a very tense scene, his friend sends him a message:

"We need to take a break."

Confused, Matías responds with another message:

"Why?"

Luciana's message doesn't take long to arrive:

"I hear a strange noise downstairs. I think Toto fell. Wait while I go to the living room to see if he's okay."
Matías sighs and pauses the movie. Toto is Luciana's dog. He is quite old and can't see well. That's why he sometimes bumps into things.

Minutes pass, and Luciana doesn't return. Matías can't resist the urge to continue watching the movie, so he messages his friend again:

"Helloooo?"

After a few seconds, he gets a response:

"Hello."

Matías starts typing:

"Is Toto okay?"

Luciana's next message makes him frown:

"It wasn't Toto."

Confused, Matías sits up in bed, but before he can type an answer, he sees another message:

"And I'm not Luciana."

Growing alarmed, Matías falls silent for a moment. He knows that his friend is also alone at her house tonight. Could she be playing a prank on him?

Yes, that has to be it. The teenager responds with another message:

"Ha ha, very funny."

Distracted while he waits for Luciana's reply, Matías doesn't hear the footsteps in the hallway until they are right behind his door. Startled, he gets up from the bed just as the door swings open:

"Hello, sweetheart!" his mother greets him. "How was your evening?"

Matías sighs relieved and feels like a true fool. A few minutes later, after his mother has left, the teenager glances at his phone again. Luciana replied:

"I thought I could scare you. Shall we continue with the movie?"

Practice

Look at the text for a minute. Then, fill out with the missing words.

Es tarde y Matías, recostado _____ su cama, mira una película _____ terror en Netflix. Al mismo tiempo, está hablando _____ Whatsapp _____ su amiga Luciana, que, desde su casa, mira la misma película.

Matías está solo _____ el departamento esta noche. Sus padres han salido _____ una cena _____ amigos. El adolescente está muy feliz _____ tener el hogar solo para él y se está divirtiendo mucho gracias _____ la película y a la conversación con Luciana.

De pronto, en medio _____ una escena muy tensa, su amiga le envía un mensaje:

"Necesitamos hacer una pausa".

Matías, confundido, responde _____ otro mensaje:

"¿Por qué?".

El mensaje _____ Luciana no tarda en llegar:

"Oigo un ruido extraño abajo. Creo que Toto se cayó. Espera mientras voy a la sala _____ ver si está bien".

Matías resopla y pausa la película. Toto es el perro _____ Luciana. Ya está muy viejo y no ve bien. _____ eso a veces se tropieza con las cosas.

Los minutos pasan y Luciana no regresa. Matías no aguanta los deseos de seguir viendo la película, de modo que vuelve a escribirle _____ su amiga:

"¿Holaaa?".

Luego _____ unos segundos, recibe una respuesta:

"Hola".
Matías se pone a escribir:

"¿Toto está bien?".

El siguiente mensaje _____ Luciana lo obliga a fruncir el ceño:

"No era Toto".

Confundido, Matías se incorpora _____ la cama, pero, antes _____ que pueda tipear una respuesta, ve otro mensaje:

"Y no soy Luciana".

Alarmado ya, Matías se queda _____ silencio por un momento. Sabe que esa noche su amiga también está sola _____ su casa. ¿Acaso le está jugando una broma?

Sí: debe ser eso. El adolescente responde _____ otro mensaje:

"Ja, ja, muy graciosa".

Distraído mientras espera la respuesta de Luciana, Matías no escucha los pasos _____ el pasillo hasta que suenan literalmente detrás _____ su puerta. Sobresaltado, se levanta de la cama al tiempo que la puerta se abre:

—¡Hola, cariño! —lo saluda su madre—. ¿Cómo estuvo tu noche?

Matías respira aliviado y se siente un verdadero ingenuo. Unos minutos después, luego _____ marcharse su madre, el adolescente vuelve a mirar el celular. Luciana contestó:

"Pensé que lograría asustarte. ¿Seguimos _____ la película?".

Go back to the original text to check your answers.

🖊 Practice a bit more!

Try to find the Spanish for the following words and expressions in the text:

a.   A horror movie: _____
b.   In the middle of: _____
c.   The urge to: _____
d.   He starts typing: _____

e. He falls silent: _____
f. Before he can: _____
g. Shall we continue with: _____

✓ Answer Key

a. *Una película de terror*
b. *En medio de*
c. *El deseo de*
d. *Se pone a escribir*
e. *Se queda en silencio*
f. *Antes de que pueda*
g. *Seguimos con*

The Difference Between Por and Para

Speakers of English usually struggle to understand the difference between Spanish prepositions *por* and *para*, but fear not! This book is here to help you!

Por usually refers to the origin, the cause or the past, whereas *para* usually refers to the future, the goal, the recipient or the destination. Let's check a few examples:

• *El regalo es **para** Lara* ("The present is for Lara").

Here, Lara is the recipient. The present goes to her. That's why we use *para*. Compare it with:

• *Vienen **por** los monumentos* ("They come for the monuments").

Here, the monuments are the cause, so they are in the past: they existed before the people came to see them. That's why we use ***por***.

Practice Time!

Read the sentences and fill out with the missing words:

a. *Compré un sérum* _____ *mi papá* ("I bought a serum for my dad").
b. *Estudio* _____ *aprender* ("I study in order to learn").
c. *No puedo comer maní* _____ *mis alergias* ("I can't eat peanuts due to my allergies").
d. *Me disculpo* _____ *mi error* ("I apologize for my mistake").
e. *Todos los días, Juan camina* _____ *el parque* ("Every day, Juan walks through the park").
f. *Este tren va* _____ *Madrid* ("This train goes to Madrid").
g. *Hice un dibujo* _____ *ti* ("I made a drawing for you").

✓ Answer Key

a.   *Compré un sérum **para** mi papá.*
b.   *Estudio **para** aprender.*
c.   *No puedo comer maní **por** mis alergias.*
d.   *Me disculpo **por** mi error.*
e.   *Todos los días, Juan camina **por** el parque.*
f.   *Este tren va **para** Madrid.*
g.   *Hice un dibujo **para** ti.*

Key Takeaways

You are doing a great job! And you've finished chapter 3, congratulations! In this chapter:

- We learned all there is to know about the most common Spanish prepositions: a, con, de, por, *para*, and *en*.
- We also talked about their uses, and we saw many examples.
- Finally, we delved into a pair of prepositions that can be a bit confusing: por and para. We learned when to use each one and how no to confuse them.

Now you know how to use the Spanish prepositions, it's time to continue with this journey. Next stop: *los sustantivos*! Chapter 4 will be dedicated to nouns and their uses!

Chapter 4: *Una casa, dos casas. Una crisis, dos...*

El objeto de la bondad no es regresarla sino propagarla.
- Julia Álvarez

Nouns

Both in English and Spanish, nouns are basic words. We use nouns to name people, things, places, or ideas. However, there are a few differences between nouns in each language. The most prominent one is gender. Let's talk a bit about that.

💬 Gender

Spanish nouns that end in -o, -e, -l, -n, and -r, are usually masculine, such as *el juego* ("the game"), *el motor* ("the engine"), and *el sol* ("the sun"). These words need masculine adjectives and articles. Nouns that end in -a, -d, -on, -z, -is, and -ie, are usually feminine, like *la playa* ("the beach"), *la felicidad* ("the happiness"), and *la canción* ("the song"). These words, on the other hand, need feminine adjectives and articles. However, there are a number of times when these rules don't work, so you can't always trust them. For some words, you might need to remember their gender by heart until you get more used to the language.

Remember what we said in Chapter 2? If a noun refers to a woman or a man (or a female or a male, if we are talking about animals), we use feminine or masculine words depending on their biological sex. In Chapter 2, we also talked about the generic masculine. This rule tells us that, if we have a group of boys and one girl, we have to use the masculine. However, if the group is made of girls only, then we use the feminine. If you want to review this topic, go back to Chapter 2, where we talk about articles and adjectives.

But guess what? Some words don't change, no matter who we are referring to. We won't get into all the rules for these special words here, but we'll show you some examples. The Spanish word for "person," that is, *la persona*, is always feminine. Therefore, if we want to say "Agustín is a good person," we have to say *Agustín es una buena persona*, where *una* ("a"), *buena* ("good") and *persona* ("person") are feminine, even if Agustín is a guy.

The same happens with *el personaje* or "the character," which is always a masculine word. If we wanted to say "Galadriel is one of the few female characters in 'The Lord of the Rings,'" what would we say? *Galadriel es uno de los pocos personajes femeninos en 'El Señor de los Anillos'*, where *uno, los, pocos, personajes,* and *femeninos* are masculine words.

💬 Number

Number is another characteristic of nouns. However, this one is a bit easier, because it's shared between English and Spanish. When it comes to most nouns, they change their form when there's more than one,

that is, when they are plural. Usually you just need to add -s or -es.

As we mentioned in Chapter 1, for most nouns and adjectives ending in -x or -s, we add -es to make them plural. But, there's a catch (or should we say a tricky rule!) — some words don't need any changes to become plural. Here are a couple of examples you might come across:

- *"El tórax" se convierte en "los tórax"* ("The thorax" becomes "the thoraces").
- *"La crisis" se convierte en "las crisis"* ("The crisis" becomes "the crises").

For a deep dive into how plurals work, head over to Chapter 1, where we talk about articles and adjectives.

Practice Time!

Read the following story:

Lucas detesta a su profesor de Matemáticas. El señor Romano es simplemente una mala persona. Todos los días elige una víctima entre los alumnos para hacerle preguntas muy difíciles frente a toda la clase. Por eso, todos los estudiantes deben prepararse mucho antes de cada lección de Matemáticas.

Hoy, Lucas ha tenido muchos problemas con la tarea y no se siente preparado para la clase en absoluto. Por lo tanto, está seguro de que el señor Romano notará sus nervios y lo elegirá como su nueva víctima.

Cuando el profesor entra a la clase, Lucas intenta ocultar la cabeza en su libro para no llamar la atención. Sin embargo, en lugar de señalar a Lucas, el profesor Romano dirige su atención hacia Tomás, el chico más tímido de la clase. El corazón de Lucas se encoge al ver a su amigo palidecer. Sabe que Tomás se pondrá aún más nervioso que él bajo la mirada penetrante del profesor.

El profesor Romano sonríe con malicia.

—Tomás, ¿puedes resolver el problema número cuatro en el pizarrón, por favor? —pregunta.

Tomás mira aterrado hacia el pizarrón. Lucas sabe que su amigo se va a bloquear y se va a sentir aún peor después de equivocarse frente a todos. No puede quedarse de brazos cruzados.

Sin pensarlo dos veces, Lucas levanta la mano y llama la atención del profesor Romano.

—¡Profesor, yo puedo intentar resolver el problema! —exclama con valentía.

El profesor Romano parece sorprendido por la intervención de Lucas, pero acepta la oferta.

Nervioso, Lucas se acerca al pizarrón y toma un marcador para comenzar. Justo cuando se está preguntando cómo saldrá de esa situación con su orgullo intacto, la alarma de incendios lo toma por sorpresa.

Como si estuvieran de acuerdo, todos los estudiantes se levantan de sus asientos y salen corriendo. Ignoran los gritos del señor Romano, que les dice que se queden quietos. Lucas decide aprovechar la oportunidad y sigue a sus compañeros. Cuando está cruzando la puerta, Tomás se acerca a él y le da un codazo de agradecimiento.

Ⓐ Translation

Now, read the translation:

Lucas hates his Math teacher. Mr. Romano is simply a bad person. Every day, he chooses a victim among the students to ask very difficult questions in front of the whole class. That's why all the students have to really prepare before each Math lesson.

Today, Lucas has struggled with his homework and feels completely unprepared for the class. Therefore, he is certain that Mr. Romano will notice his nervousness and choose him as his new victim.

As the teacher enters the classroom, Lucas tries to bury his head in his book to avoid drawing attention. However, instead of singling out Lucas, Mr. Romano directs his gaze towards Tomás, the shyest boy in the class. Lucas's heart sinks as he watches his friend grow paler. He knows Tomás will become even more nervous under the penetrating gaze of the teacher.

Mr. Romano smiles maliciously.

"Tomás, can you solve problem number four on the board, please?" he asks.

Terrified, Tomás looks towards the board. Lucas knows his friend will freeze and he will feel even worse after making a mistake in front of everyone. He can't stand idly by.

Without a second thought, Lucas raises his hand and catches Mr. Romano's attention.

"Sir, I can try to solve the problem!" he exclaims courageously.

Mr. Romano seems surprised by Lucas's intervention, but he accepts the offer.

Nervously, Lucas walks towards the board and grabs a marker to begin. Just as he is wondering how to save his pride from the situation, the fire alarm catches him off guard.

As if they are on it together, all the students stand up from their seats and rush out. They ignore Mr. Romano's shouts for them to remain calm. Lucas decides to seize the opportunity and follows his classmates. When he is crossing the door, Tomás approaches him and gives a thankful elbow nudge.

Practice!

Add an article and an adjective to the following nouns. You can use the same adjective more than once. Don't forget to change the articles' and adjectives' gender! The first one it's done as an example.

a.   víctima: *la víctima nueva*
b.   *estudiante:* _____
c.   *problema:* _____
d.   *atención:* _____
e.   *persona:* _____
f.   *amigo:* _____
g.   *presión:* _____

✓ Key (possible answers):

a.   *una víctima nueva*
b.   *el estudiante aterrado* or *la estudiante aterrada*
c.   *un problema pequeño*
d.   *una atención pequeña*
e.   *la persona buena*
f.   *el amigo feliz*
g.   *la presión grande*

Key Takeaways

You are a very persistent person! And now you've finished chapter 4, congratulations! In this chapter:

- You've learned everything about Spanish nouns and how they change in gender and number.
- You've also learned that some nouns don't vary in gender, such as *el personaje* ("the character").
- Finally, you've learned a bit more about how to change adjectives according to the noun they are describing.

Are you ready for the next chapter? There, you'll be learning everything you need to know about personal pronouns! Did you know that Spanish speakers have five different words for "you"? Keep reading and find out more!

Chapter 5: *Tú y yo*

Poesía eres tú.
- Gustavo Adolfo Bécquer

Subject Personal Pronouns

In the following table, you'll find the subject personal pronouns of Spanish with their English counterparts. These pronouns are the ones we use as a subject instead of a noun.

Yo	I
Tú / Usted / Vos	You (singular)
Él	He
Ella	She
Nosotros (masculine) *Nosotras (feminine)*	We
Ustedes	You (plural)
Ellos (masculine) *Ellas (feminine)*	They

In some cases, we have more than one Spanish pronoun for an English one. Why? Well, we'll talk about this in the next section.

💬 *Tú*, *vos* or *usted*?

The forms *tú* and *vos* are actually just regional variations. While the specifics of their usage aren't within the scope of this book, it's important to understand that they're essentially equivalent, although they typically pair with different verb forms or conjugations.

However, what's particularly relevant for us is the contrast between *tú* (or *vos*) and *usted*. Even though certain countries lean towards using *usted* more frequently, while others use it only sporadically, there are general guidelines to consider.

Usted is the formal way of addressing someone in Spanish. Though formality and informality can vary based on social norms and geographic factors, *usted* is generally employed when addressing strangers, individuals who are older (especially if you are not close to them), or people in a higher position within a hierarchy. For instance, to ask a stranger on the street for the time, you might say, *¿Puede usted decirme la hora, por favor?* (Literally, "May you tell me the time, please?").

Tú (and *vos*), on the other hand, are used in informal contexts, with family and friends, and to address younger people.

Dropping the Pronoun

Compared to English, Spanish has a broader range of verb forms. These verb forms allow us to guess who the subject is without having to explicitly state it. So, in Spanish, it's possible (and advisable) to omit the subject pronoun at the beginning of a sentence. Adding the pronoun can alter the sentence's meaning. We only add them when context dictates it's necessary.

Here are some examples:
- *Eres inteligente* ("You are smart," with no other meanings).
- *Tú eres inteligente* (Could be emphatic or express contrast, as in, "You are smart and he is not").

Therefore, the lesson here is simple: omit the pronoun unless there's a clear reason to include it. And which situations demand a pronoun?

- Potential ambiguity: Imagine a scenario where there are three people. One of them is your superior, and you need to address them using usted. The verb conjugation for usted is the same as for él and ella. Therefore, to avoid ambiguity, adding the pronoun clarifies who you're referring to:
  Es amable (This can be translated to "You are kind," "He is kind," or "She is kind").
  Usted es amable ("You are kind").
  Él es amable ("He is kind").
- Emphasis:
  Tú sí que eres fastidioso ("You are annoying!").
- Contrast:
  Tú eres una buena persona. Él no ("You are a good person. He isn't").

Practice Time!

Read the following story:

Julia sale temprano de la escuela y decide ir a su tienda de cómics favorita para comprar algunos mangas. Mientras ojea los nuevos títulos y busca el tomo número 11 de la saga que está leyendo, el sonido de unas voces familiares llama su atención:

—¿Estás seguro? —pregunta un chico adolescente que está entrando a la tienda.

—Te digo que sí. Aquí lo encontraremos —insiste otro chico que viene detrás del primero.

Julia no puede creer su mala suerte: se trata de Adrián y Santiago, dos chicos de su clase que siempre la molestan. ¿Qué están haciendo en su tienda favorita?

Ellos no la han visto y se dirigen rápidamente al mostrador para hablar con el vendedor:

—Disculpe, señor —saluda Adrián—. ¿Usted sabe si ya llegó el tomo número 10 de Sakamoto Deizu?

—*Lo siento, chicos: ya está agotado —se disculpa el vendedor.*

Desilusionados, Adrián y Santiago dejan escapar varias expresiones de enfado.

—*¡No puede ser! ¡Es la tercera tienda que visitamos! —se queja Santiago—. ¿No sabe en dónde podemos conseguirlo?*

—*Todo el mundo lo ha leído menos nosotros —explica Adrián.*

—*Será difícil —suspira el vendedor—. Creo que ya no nos queda en ninguna sucursal.*

Aunque Julia está dándoles la espalda a sus compañeros para evitar que la reconozcan, escucha toda la conversación. Se pregunta cómo Adrián y Santiago pueden ser tan tontos: hace semanas que ella leyó el tomo número 10 de Sakamoto Deizu en internet. No es difícil de encontrar. Sin embargo, tiene que admitir que es extraño que dos chicos tan poco inteligentes tengan buen gusto en mangas.

—*¿No puede fijarse en la computadora? —le insiste Santiago al vendedor.*

—*Puedo intentar —responde el hombre—, pero ¿saben algo?
Si tienen prisa por leerlo, pueden buscar en internet.*

—*¡Ya buscamos! —gruñe Santiago—. No está en ningún lado.*

Julia ahoga la risa: claramente no saben en qué páginas web buscar.

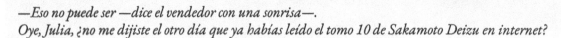

—*Eso no puede ser —dice el vendedor con una sonrisa—.
Oye, Julia, ¿no me dijiste el otro día que ya habías leído el tomo 10 de Sakamoto Deizu en internet?*

Descubierta, Julia se muerde los labios y siente los ojos de sus compañeros en la nuca.

—*¿Es Julia? —susurra sorprendido Santiago.*

No hay forma de escapar: la han descubierto. Intentando no lucir asustada, se da vuelta y ve que los dos chicos no parecen contentos de encontrarla allí.

—*Sí —contesta, seria—. Es fácil de encontrar, si uno sabe dónde buscar.*

—*Bueno: en ese caso, podrías ayudarnos, ¿o no? —sugiere Santiago, mientras se cruza de brazos.*

—*Yo no ayudo a los bravucones —contesta Julia. Luego, se acerca al mostrador para pagar sus mangas.*

—*¡Siempre eres tan antipática! —se queja Santiago—. Ya ves por qué a nadie le agradas.*

Julia respira hondo y mantiene la calma, aunque por dentro se siente muy tensa.

—*Vamos, niños: esas cosas no se dicen —interviene el vendedor, confundido—. Tal vez, si Julia los ayuda, ustedes puedan prometer no molestarla más.*

—*Nunca la molestamos. Está exagerando —miente Santiago.*

—*Vamos, Julia, no seas tan rencorosa: son solo algunas bromas —sonríe Adrián, que quiere calmar la situación—. Llevamos mucho tiempo buscando este manga. Al menos dinos en dónde podemos leerlo.*

—*¿De verdad quieren saber?*

—*¡Sí! —contestan los dos.*

—*Muy bien: les diré... En una semana, si dejan de molestarme.*

(A) Translation

Now, read the translation:

Julia leaves school early and decides to go to her favorite comic book store to buy some manga. As she browses the new titles, looking for volume 11 of the series she is reading, the sound of familiar voices catch her attention:

"Are you sure?" a teenage boy asks as he enters the store.

"Yes, I'm telling you. We'll find it here," insists another boy behind him.

Julia can't believe her bad luck: they are Adrián and Santiago, two boys from her class who always bother her. What are they doing in her favorite store?

They haven't seen her and they quickly head to the counter to talk to the clerk:

"Excuse me, sir," asks Adrián, "do you know if volume 10 of *Sakamoto Deizu* has arrived?"

"I'm sorry, guys, it's already sold out," the clerk apologizes.

Disappointed, Adrián and Santiago let out some frustration phrases.

"I can't believe it! This is the third store we've visited," complains Santiago. "Don't you know where we can get it?"

"Everyone has read it except for us," explains Adrián.

"It's going to be difficult," the clerk sighs. "I think we're out of stock in all of our branches."

Although Julia has her back turned to her classmates to avoid being recognized, she hears the entire conversation. She wonders how Adrián and Santiago can be so clueless: she read volume 10 of *Saka-*

moto Deizu online weeks ago. It isn't hard to find. However, she has to admit it is strange that two not-so-bright guys have good taste in manga.

"Can't you check on the computer?" insists Santiago, talking to the clerk.

"I can try," answers the man, "but you know what? If you're in a hurry to read it, you can look online."

"We've already looked!" grumbles Santiago. "It's nowhere to be found."

Julia stifles her laughter: they clearly don't know where to look on the internet.

"That can't be right," says the clerk, smiling. "Hey, Julia, didn't you tell me the other day that you had already read volume 10 of *Sakamoto Deizu* online?"

Busted, Julia bites her lip and feels her classmates' eyes on her.

"Is that Julia?" whispers Santiago, surprised.

There is no way to escape: they have seen her. Trying not to look scared, she turns around and sees that the two boys don't seem pleased to find her there.

"Yes," she replies, seriously. "It's easy to find, if you know where to look."

"Well, in that case, you could help us, right?" suggests Santiago, crossing his arms.

"I don't help bullies," replies Julia, stepping closer to the counter to pay for her manga.

"You're always so obnoxious!" Santiago complains. "Now you see why no one likes you."

Julia takes a deep breath and stays calm, although she feels very tense inside.

"Come on, kids, you shouldn't say things like that," intervenes the clerk, confused. "Maybe if Julia helps you, you could promise not to bother her anymore."

"We never bother her. She's exaggerating," lies Santiago.

"Come on, Julia, don't be so resentful: they're just a few jokes," says Adrián, smiling, trying to defuse the situation. "We've been looking for this manga for a long time. At least tell us where we can read it."

"Do you really want to know?"

"Yes!" answer both of them.

"Alright then, I'll tell you... In a week, if you stop bothering me."

Practice!

1. Go back to the text and underline all the personal pronouns you can find.
2. Can you spot an instance where someone uses usted instead of tú? Why is that?
3. Go back to the text again. With the help of the translation, highlight at least 10 instances of dropped pronouns, that is, instances where the verb doesn't have an explicit subject.

Answer Key

Julia sale temprano de la escuela y decide ir a su tienda de cómics favorita para comprar algunos mangas. Mientras ojea los nuevos títulos y busca el tomo número 11 de la saga que está leyendo, el sonido de unas voces familiares llama su atención:

—¿Estás seguro? —pregunta un chico adolescente que está entrando a la tienda.

—Te digo que sí. Aquí lo encontraremos —insiste otro chico que viene detrás del primero.

Julia no puede creer su mala suerte: se trata de Adrián y Santiago, dos chicos de su clase que siempre la molestan. ¿Qué están haciendo en su tienda favorita?

Ellos no la han visto y se dirigen rápidamente al mostrador para hablar con el vendedor:

—Disculpe, señor —saluda Adrián—. ¿Usted sabe si ya llegó el tomo número 10 de Sakamoto Deizu?

—Lo siento, chicos: ya está agotado —se disculpa el vendedor.

Desilusionados, Adrián y Santiago dejan escapar varias expresiones de enfado.

—¡No puede ser! ¡Es la tercera tienda que visitamos! —se queja Santiago—. ¿No sabe en dónde podemos conseguirlo?

—Todo el mundo lo ha leído menos nosotros —explica Adrián.

—Será difícil —suspira el vendedor—. Creo que ya no nos queda en ninguna sucursal.

Aunque Julia está dándoles la espalda a sus compañeros para evitar que la reconozcan, escucha toda la conversación. Se pregunta cómo Adrián y Santiago pueden ser tan tontos: hace semanas que ella leyó el tomo número 10 de Sakamoto Deizu en internet. No es difícil de encontrar. Sin embargo, tiene que admitir que es extraño que dos chicos tan poco inteligentes tengan buen gusto en mangas.

—¿No puede fijarse en la computadora? —le insiste Santiago al vendedor.

—Puedo intentar —responde el hombre—, pero ¿saben algo? Si tienen prisa por leerlo, pueden buscar en internet.

—¡Ya buscamos! —gruñe Santiago—. No está en ningún lado.
Julia ahoga la risa: claramente no saben en qué páginas web buscar.

—*Eso no puede ser* —*dice el vendedor con una sonrisa*—. *Oye, Julia, ¿tú no me dijiste el otro día que ya habías leído el tomo 10 de* Sakamoto Deizu *en internet?*

Descubierta, Julia se muerde los labios y siente los ojos de sus compañeros en la nuca.

—*¿Es Julia?* —*susurra sorprendido Santiago.*

No hay forma de escapar: la han descubierto. Intentando no lucir asustada, se da vuelta y ve que los dos chicos no parecen contentos de encontrarla allí.

—*Sí* —*contesta, seria*—. *Es fácil de encontrar, si uno sabe dónde buscar.*

—*Bueno: en ese caso, podrías ayudarnos, ¿o no?* —*sugiere Santiago, mientras se cruza de brazos.*

—*No ayudo a los bravucones* —*contesta Julia. Luego, se acerca al mostrador para pagar sus mangas.*

—*¡Siempre eres tan antipática!* —*se queja Santiago*—. *Ya ves por qué a nadie le agradas.*

Julia respira hondo y mantiene la calma, aunque por dentro se siente muy tensa.

—*Vamos, niños: esas cosas no se dicen* —*interviene el vendedor, confundido*—. *Tal vez, si Julia los ayuda, ustedes puedan prometer no molestarla más.*

—*Nunca la molestamos. Está exagerando* —*miente Santiago.*

—*Vamos, Julia, no seas tan rencorosa: son solo algunas bromas* —*sonríe Adrián, que quiere calmar la situación*—. *Llevamos mucho tiempo buscando este manga. Al menos dinos en dónde podemos leerlo.*

—*¿De verdad quieren saber?*

—*¡Sí!* —*contestan los dos.*

—*Muy bien: les diré... En una semana, si dejan de molestarme.*

The boys refer to the clerk as *usted* because they don't know him and he is older.

Key Takeaways

Congratulations on finishing chapter 5! This was a hard one, but you still made it through!

So what have you learned?
- Spanish personal pronouns and how to use them.
- How to say "you" in Spanish, according to number and level of formality.
- How and when to drop the pronouns.

Now that you know how to use the personal pronouns, the next step is to learn how to use the verbs!

Chapter 6: *Soy mexicano, pero estoy en Estados Unidos*

En algún lugar de un libro hay una frase esperándonos para darle un sentido a la existencia.
- Miguel de Cervantes

Verbs and Adverbs

In this chapter, we'll deal with two very important parts of speech: los *verbos* ("verbs") and *los adverbios* ("adverbs"). Spanish verbs have a bad reputation, but there is no need to fear: we'll go step by step, learning the most basic ones. Are you ready?

Verbs *Ser* and *Estar*

The verbs *ser* and *estar* can't be easily translated into English. Both of them mean "to be," but they're used in different situations. Let's check their differences.

💬 *Ser*

Let's start by conjugating the verb *ser* in the present simple.

Yo soy	I am
Tú eres / Usted es	You are (singular)
Él / Ella es	He / she is
Nosotros somos	we are
Ustedes son	You are (plural)
Ellos / Ellas son	They are

This verb is used to talk about things that are permanent, essential, or inherent to someone or something. It's often used to describe someone's identity, physical characteristics, nationality, profession, and more. Here are a few examples:

- Identity: *Soy Juan* ("I am Juan") or *Eres su mamá* ("You are his mom").
- Physical characteristics: *Ella es alta* ("She is tall") or *El perro es blanco* ("The dog is white").
- Nationality, religion or political orientation: *Somos españoles* ("We are Spanish"), *Son católicas* ("They are Catholic") or *Son liberales* ("They are liberals").
- Profession: *Mi padre es médico* ("My father is a doctor") or *Ella es profesora* ("She is a teacher").

The verb *ser* implies something that doesn't change quickly or easily. It's about who or what something fundamentally is.

💬 *Estar*

Estar, on the other hand, is used to talk about temporary states, conditions, or locations. First, let's conjugate the verb:

Yo estoy	I am
Tú estás / Usted está	You are (singular)
Él / Ella está	He / she is
Nosotros somos	we are
Ustedes son	You are (plural)
Ellos / Ellas son	They are

We use *estar* for things that can change or vary over time. It's about how something is in a particular moment. Here are some examples:

- Temporary conditions or emotions: *Estoy cansado* ("I am tired") or *Estamos enamorados* ("We are in love").
- Location: *Estoy en casa* ("I am home") or *Los libros están en la mesa* ("The books are on the table").
- Health: *Mi hermana está enferma* ("My sister is sick").

It might seem a bit confusing at first, especially when deciding whether to use *ser* or *estar*. But, as you practice and you get familiar with different contexts, you'll start to get the hang of it. Just remember that we use *ser* for things that are permanent, like identity and characteristics, while we use estar for temporary states and conditions.

Learning when to use these two verbs is an important step in mastering Spanish, and with practice, you'll become more confident in choosing the right one in each situation!

Practice Time!

Read the sentences and choose the correct verb: *ser* or *estar*. You can use the translations below to help you!

a. *Guido* **es** / **está** *el novio de Verónica.*
b. *Mi casa* **es** / **está** *en la playa.*
c. *Tú* **eres** / **estás** *muy inteligente.*
d. *Martín no* **es** / **está** *en Madrid:* **es** / **está** *en Bogotá.*
e. *Ana* **es** / **está** *judía.*
f. *Este libro* **es** / **está** *de Antonio.*
g. *Buenos Aires* **es** / **está** *una ciudad.*
h. *Buenos Aires* **es** / **está** *en Argentina.*
i. *Queremos estudiar, pero* **somos** / **estamos** *cansados.*
j. *¡El profesor de teatro me eligió a mí! ¡* **Soy** / **estoy** *Hamlet en la obra!*
k. *Adriana* **es** / **está** *quien nos cuida.*

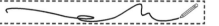

(A) Translation

a.   Guido is Veronica's boyfriend.
b.   My house is on the beach.
c.   You are very intelligent.
d.   Martín is not in Madrid: he is in Bogotá.
e.   Ana is Jewish.
f.   This book belongs to Antonio.
g.   Buenos Aires is a city.
h.   Buenos Aires is in Argentina.
i.   We want to study, but we are tired.
j.   The theater teacher chose me! I am Hamlet in the play!
k.   Adriana is the one who takes care of us.

(✓) Answer Key

a.   *Guido **es** el novio de Verónica*
b.   *Mi casa **está** en la playa.*
c.   *Tú **eres** muy inteligente.*
d.   *Martín no **está** en Madrid: **está** en Bogotá.*
e.   *Ana **es** judía.*
f.   *Este libro **es** de Antonio.*
g.   *Buenos Aires **es** una ciudad.*
h.   *Buenos Aires **está** en Argentina.*
i.   *Queremos estudiar, pero **estamos** cansados.*
j.   *¡El profesor de teatro me eligió a mí! ¡**Soy** Hamlet en la obra!*
k.   *Adriana **es** quien nos cuida.*

The verb *Tener*

The Spanish verb *tener* means "to have." It's used to express possession or ownership of things. Let's break it down a bit:

1.   Conjugation:

Yo tengo	I have
Tú tienes / Usted tiene	You have (singular)
Él / Ella tiene	He / she has
Nosotros tenemos	We have
Ustedes tienen	You have (plural)
Ellos / Ellas tienen	They have

2. Basic Meaning: Possession

Tener is used to talk about things that you have or possess. Just like in English, it shows ownership. Here are a few examples:

- *Tengo un perro* ("I have a dog").
- *Ella tiene un auto nuevo* ("She has a new car").
- *¿Tienes un lápiz?* ("Do you have a pencil?").

3. Age

In Spanish, the verb *tener* is also used to express age:

- Tengo veinte años ("I am twenty years old").
- Mi hermano tiene diez años ("My brother is ten years old").

It's very common to forget this use of *tener* and to use one of the equivalents of the verb "to be." But in Spanish, age is expressed with the verb *tener*, not with *ser* or *estar*.

4. Feelings and Emotions

Tener can also be used to describe feelings, sensations, and states. Let's check some examples:

- *Tengo hambre* ("I am hungry").
- *Ella tiene sueño* ("She is sleepy").
- *Nosotros tenemos miedo* ("We are scared").

5. Other Expressions

Additionally, tener is part of some common expressions in Spanish. For example:

- *Tener éxito* ("To be successful").
- *Tener cuidado* ("To be careful").
- *Tener razón* ("To be right").

So, *tener* is a versatile verb that helps you talk about possession, age, feelings, and more in Spanish. It's one of the building blocks of the language, and you'll use it a lot when speaking and writing in Spanish.

Practice Time!

Read the following text and fill in the gaps with the correct verb. Choose between *ser*, *estar* and *tener*. You can use the translation for help. Don't forget to conjugate the verbs!

Luisa _____ mi mejor amiga de la escuela. Su casa _____ al lado de la mía. Ella _____ dos hermanos: Lucas y Andrea. Andrea _____ dos años y Lucas, siete.

Luisa _____ alta y _____ el cabello castaño y rizado. Lucas _____ bajito y _____ el cabello rubio y corto. Andrea _____ casi un bebé y se parece a todos los otros bebés.

Además, Luisa _____ un gato llamado Atún, que _____ marrón, blanco y muy gordo. Atún siempre _____ durmiendo sobre la cama de mi amiga. Cuando se despierta, maulla muy fuerte, porque siempre _____ hambre.

Luisa siempre _____ contenta cuando la visito, pero su hermano Lucas no. Mientras nosotras jugamos, él se va a su cuarto, que _____ azul y grande. _____ una televisión y muchos videojuegos, pero nunca quiere compartirlos.

Los papás de Luisa se llaman Santiago y Diana. Diana _____ psicóloga y Santiago _____ diseñador gráfico.

Me encanta visitar a la familia de Luisa. _____ una de mis actividades preferidas.

Ⓐ Translation

Luisa is my best friend from school. Her house is next to mine. She has two siblings: Lucas and Andrea. Andrea is two years old and Lucas is seven.

Luisa is tall and has brown, curly hair. Lucas is short and has short, blonde hair. Andrea is almost a baby and she looks like all other babies.

Luisa also has a cat named Atún, which is brown, white, and very fat. Atún is always sleeping on my friend's bed. When Atún wakes up, he meows very loudly because he's always hungry.

Luisa is always happy when I visit her, but her brother Lucas isn't. While we play, he goes to his room, which is big and blue. He has a TV and a lot of video games, but he never wants to share them.

Luisa's parents are called Santiago and Diana. Diana is a psychologist and Santiago is a graphic designer. I love visiting Luisa's family. It's one of my favorite activities.

Ⓥ Answer Key

*Luisa **es** mi mejor amiga de la escuela. Su casa **está** al lado de la mía. Ella **tiene** dos hermanos: Lucas y Andrea. Andrea **tiene** dos años y Lucas, siete.*

*Luisa **es** alta y **tiene** el cabello castaño y rizado. Lucas **es** bajito y **tiene** el cabello rubio y corto. Andrea **es** casi un bebé y se parece a todos los otros bebés.*

*Además, Luisa **tiene** un gato llamado Atún, que **es** marrón, blanco y muy gordo. Atún siempre **está** durmiendo sobre la cama de mi amiga. Cuando se despierta, maulla muy fuerte, porque siempre **tiene** hambre.*

*Luisa siempre **está** contenta cuando la visito, pero su hermano Lucas no. Mientras nosotras jugamos, él se va a su cuarto, que **es** azul y grande. **Tiene** una televisión y muchos videojuegos, pero nunca quiere prestarlos.*

*Los papás de Luisa se llaman Santiago y Diana. Diana **es** psicóloga y Santiago es diseñador gráfico.*

*Me encanta visitar a la familia de Luisa. **Es** una de mis actividades preferidas.*

Other verbs

The Three Regular Conjugations: verbs ending in -ar, -er, and -ir

In Spanish, there are three regular verb conjugations, which work like a pattern to modify the form of a verb so that it matches the subject (who is doing the action) and the tense (when the action is happening). These conjugations are based on the ending of the verb.

Here are the three verb conjugations:

💬 -AR Verbs:

In this group, we find the verbs that end in *-ar*, like *hablar* ("to speak"). When you want to conjugate a regular verb ending in *-ar*, you have to change the *-ar* ending for another one, agreeing with the subject and tense. Let's see how this works with the verb *hablar*.

- *Yo habl**o*** ("I speak").
- *Tú habl**as*** ("You speak").
- *Usted habl**a*** ("You speak").
- *Él/Ella habl**a*** ("He/She speaks").
- *Nosotros/Nosotras habl**amos*** ("We speak").
- *Ustedes/Ellos/Ellas habl**an*** ("You/They speak").

What you see in bold in each case is the ending you add after dropping the *-ar* ending so that the verb agrees in person and number with the subject. See how the verb *amar* ("to love") changes in the exact same way:

- *Yo am**o*** ("I love").
- *Tú am**as*** ("You love").
- *Usted am**a*** ("You love").
- *Él/Ella am**a*** ("He/She loves").
- *Nosotros/Nosotras am**amos*** ("We love").
- *Ustedes/Ellos/Ellas am**an*** ("You/They love").

💬 -ER Verbs:

These are verbs that end in *-er*, like *comer* ("to eat"). Just like *-ar* verbs, you change the ending to match the subject and tense. For example:

- *Yo com**o*** ("I eat").
- *Tú com**es*** ("You eat").
- *Usted com**e*** ("You eat").
- *Él/Ella com**e*** ("He/She eats").

- *Nosotros/Nosotras com**emos*** ("We eat").
- *Ustedes/Ellos/Ellas com**en*** ("You/They eat").

Again, the endings in bold are the ones you'll have to add after dropping the *-er* to conjugate in the present tense any regular *-er* verb.

💬 -IR Verbs:

These are verbs that end in *-ir*, like *vivir* ("to live"). Once more, you change the ending based on the subject and tense. Let's check it:

- Yo vivo ("I live").
- Tú vives ("You live").
- Usted vive ("You live").
- Él/Ella vive ("He/She lives").
- Nosotros/Nosotras vivimos ("We live").
- Ustedes/Ellos/Ellas viven ("You/They live").

So, the key is to recognize the verb's ending in its infinitive form (*-ar*, *-er*, or *-ir*) and then apply the correct conjugation pattern to match the situation. These regular verb conjugations are the foundation for building sentences in Spanish.

Practice Time!

Read the sentences and fill in the gaps with the correct conjugation of the verb in brackets. Use the translation to help you.

a.   Yo _____ *(hablar) inglés* ("I speak English").
b.   Tú _____ *(comer) pizza* ("You eat pizza").
c.   Él _____ *(leer) un libro* ("He reads a book").
d.   Ella _____ *(bailar) bien* ("She dances well").
e.   Nosotros _____ *(estudiar) mucho* ("We study a lot").
f.   Ustedes _____ *(practicar) fútbol* ("You all play soccer").
g.   Ellos _____ *(cantar) en el coro* ("They sing in the choir").
h.   Usted _____ *(trabajar) aquí* ("You work here").
i.   Ellas _____ *(nadar) en la piscina* ("They swim in the pool").
j.   Lila _____ *(escribir) muchos cuentos* ("Lila writes a lot of short stories").

✓ Answer Key

a.   Yo **hablo** *inglés.*
b.   Tú **comes** *pizza.*
c.   Él **lee** *un libro.*
d.   Ella **baila** *bien.*
e.   Nosotros **estudiamos** *mucho.*
f.   Ustedes **practican** *fútbol.*

g.   *Ellos **cantan** en el coro.*
h.   *Usted **trabaja** aquí.*
i.   *Ellas **nadan** en la piscina.*
j.   *Lila **escribe** muchos cuentos.*

Adverbs

Adverbs are words that modify adjectives, verbs, or other adverbs. They express relationships of time, place, cause, manner, and degree, among others. There are several categories of adverbs in Spanish. Here, we'll focus on the most frequent ones!

1.   The negative adverb *no*:

If you want to build a negative statement in Spanish, all you have to do is add the word *no* before the verb. Let's take a look at some examples:

- *Tracey habla español* ("Tracey speaks Spanish").
- *Tracey **no** habla español* ("Tracey doesn't speak Spanish").
- *Quiero pizza* ("I want pizza").
- ***No** quiero pizza* ("I don't want pizza").

Pretty easy, right?

2.   Frequency adverbs:

The good thing about these adverbs is that you can place them anywhere in the sentence. Let's check the most frequent ones:

- *Siempre* ("always")
- *Usualmente/normalmente* ("usually")
- *Con frecuencia* ("often/frequently")
- *A veces* ("sometimes")
- *Casi nunca* ("hardly ever")
- *Nunca* ("never")

Modal adverbs:

They are equivalent to the English adverbs that end in -ly. In Spanish, they tend to end in *-mente*. In both languages, they normally come from an adjective, to which we add the -ly or *-mente* ending. Whenever the adjective originating the adverb has a masculine gender marker (*-o*), you need to change it into an *-a* before adding *-mente* to form the adverb. Let's check a few examples.

- *feliz + -mente = felizmente* ("happily")
- *triste + -mente = tristemente* ("sadly")
- *rápido + -mente = rápidamente* ("quickly")

However, some very common adverbs don't end in *-mente*. The most important examples are:

- *Bien* ("well")
- *Mal* ("badly")

Also, be careful not to overuse adverbs ending in *-mente*, since Spanish has a lower tolerance for modal adverbs than English.

Practice Time!

Fill in the gaps with the correct Spanish adverbs:

ENGLISH		SPANISH	
easy	easily	*fácil*	
brilliant	brillianty	*brillante*	
high	highly	*alto*	
funny	funnily	*gracioso*	
literal	literally	*literal*	
practical	practically	*práctico*	
normal	normally	*normal*	

⊘ Answer Key

Fácilmente, brillantemente, altamente, graciosamente, literalmente, prácticamente, normalmente.

Key Takeaways

You have arrived at the end of Chapter 6! Good for you!

Thanks to your efforts, you have learned:

- Three super important Spanish verbs: *ser, estar* and *tener*.
- How to conjugate those three irregular verbs.
- How to conjugate regular verbs in the present simple.
- All about Spanish adverbs and how to use them.

We've covered a lot so far, but we're still missing one type of word! Oh, my God, say hello to the interjections!

Chapter 7: *¡Oye, tú!*

Tú, que me lees, ¿estás seguro de entender mi idioma?
- Jorge Luis Borges

Interjections

So, what is an interjection? It's a type of word or expression that conveys a strong and immediate emotion, reaction, or feeling. Interjections are often used to express surprise, excitement, joy, frustration, pain, agreement, disagreement, or other intense emotion in a sentence. They are typically short and they stand alone, separated from the rest of the sentence structure. Interjections are used to add emphasis or convey the speaker's emotional response to a situation. Some examples of interjections in English are "Wow!" or "Ouch!"

💬 Proper Interjections

By "proper interjections" we mean those that don't include full words. Here is a list of some of the most common ones. In brackets, you'll find the closest English equivalent.

- *¡Ah!* ("ah!," "huh!," "oh!"): we use it to express amazement, surprise or pleasure.
- *¡Oh!* ("oh!"): we use it to express amazement or admiration.
- *¡Ay!* ("ouch!," "oh!"): we use it to express sudden pain.
- *¿Eh?, ¡eh!* ("huh?," "huh!," "hey!"): it's used to ask for clarification, and to express anger or rejection.
- *¡Ey!* ("hey!"): we use it as a way of warning.
- *¡Uy!* ("oh!"): it expresses amazement or surprise.
- *¡Puaj!* ("yuck!"): we use it to express disgust.
- *¡Uf!, ¡fiuf!* ("phew!"): it's used to express relief or tiredness.
- *¡Bah!* ("bah!"): it expresses disdain.

💬 Other Interjections

The following interjections do have full words:

- *¡Dios mío!* ("oh my God!")
- *¡Por amor de Dios!, ¡por el amor de Dios!* ("for the love of God!")
- *¡Cuidado!* ("watch out!," "careful!")
- *¡Ojo!* ("be careful!," "beware!"): this one can express either a warning or a threat.
- *¡Hombre!, ¡mujer!* ("man!," "woman!")
- *¡Oye!* ("hey!")
- *¡Vaya!* ("wow!"): it comes from the verb "to go."

Practice Time!

Read the following text and underline every interjection you find. Use the translation to help you!

—¡Cuidado, Lucas! —exclama Catalina, asustada.

—¡Bah! —responde su hermano Lucas, que, recostado en la calle, tiene un brazo dentro de la alcantarilla.

En ese momento, una mujer sale de una tienda, los ve y corre hacia ellos preocupada:

—¡Eh, ustedes dos! ¿Qué están haciendo? —quiere saber, alarmada.

—Hay un gatito atrapado en el alcantarillado —le explica Catalina—. Lo oímos cuando volvíamos de la escuela, y mi hermano está tratando de salvarlo.

—¡Oh, no! —se espanta la mujer—. ¡Pobrecito!

—Ya casi lo tengo —les avisa Lucas, todavía concentrado en su tarea—. Está asustado y no me deja sujetarlo.

—Deberíamos llamar a los bomberos —sugiere la mujer, sin saber qué hacer.

—Eso no servirá —dice Lucas—. El brazo de un adulto no cabe por aquí. ¡Ay, ni siquiera el mío cabe! Catalina, tu brazo es más pequeño: deberías intentarlo tú.

—¡Puaj! —exclama Catalina—. La alcantarilla está muy sucia...

—¿Quieres salvar al gatito o no? —le pregunta su hermano.

Catalina suspira: en efecto, la idea de ese pobre gatito atrapado la llena de pena. Está dispuesta a hacer algo tan asqueroso como meter su brazo en esa sucia alcantarilla para salvarlo. Más tarde puede lavarse en casa. Y lavar al gatito, también.

Decidida, se arrodilla en la calle junto a su hermano y mete el brazo. Luego de unos momentos, siente el pecho del gatito e intenta sujetarlo con gentileza. Tiene que operar muy lentamente, teme hacerle daño al pobre bebé, que forcejea muy asustado.

Finalmente, en cuanto el gatito deja de moverse por un segundo, Catalina aprovecha la oportunidad y sube el brazo, que emerge de la alcantarilla con un gatito color gris.

—¡Oh, Dios mío: es precioso! —exclama la mujer, conmovida—. ¡Pobrecito! Hay que llevarlo al veterinario.

Los niños le dicen que su madre es veterinaria, así que van a llevarlo a su casa. Su madre puede revisarlo y asegurarse de que está bien. Por lo tanto, luego de despedirse de la señora, Catalina y Lucas corren a casa junto al pequeño rescatado.

A Translation

"Careful, Lucas!" exclaims Catalina, alarmed.

"Oh, relax," answers her brother Lucas, who is leaning over the street with his arm inside the sewer. At that moment, a woman comes out of a store, sees them, and rushes over, concerned.

"Hey, you two! What are you doing?" she asks, alarmed.

"There's a kitten trapped in the sewer," explains Catalina. "We heard it when we were coming back from school, and my brother is trying to save it."

"Oh, no!" the woman gasps. "Poor thing!"

"I'm almost there," Lucas informs them, still focused on his task. "It's scared and won't let me grab it." "We should call the firefighters," suggests the woman, not knowing what to do.

"That won't work," says Lucas. "An adult's arm doesn't fit through here. Heck, not even mine fits! Catalina, your arm is smaller; you should try."

"Ew," exclaims Catalina. "The sewer is really dirty."

"Do you want to save the kitten or not?" her brother asks her.

Catalina sighs; indeed, the thought of that poor kitten trapped fills her with sadness. She is willing to do something as disgusting as putting her arm in that filthy sewer to save it. She can wash up at home later. And wash the kitten, too.

Determined, she kneels on the street beside her brother and inserts her arm. After a few moments, she feels the kitten's chest and tries to gently grab it. She has to proceed very slowly because she is afraid of hurting the poor thing, who is frightened and struggling.

Finally, when the kitten stops moving for a second, Catalina takes the chance and pulls her arm out of the sewer, along with a gray kitten.

"Oh, my goodness, it's adorable!" exclaims the woman . "Poor thing! We need to take it to the vet."

The children tell her that their mother is a veterinarian, so they will take the kitten home. Their mother can check it and make sure it's okay. So, after saying goodbye to the lady, Catalina and Lucas rush home with their little rescue.

✓ Answer Key

—¡*Cuidado*, Lucas! —*exclama Catalina, asustada.*

—¡*Bah*! —*responde su hermano Lucas, que, recostado en la calle, tiene un brazo dentro de la alcantarilla.*

A. Translation

"Careful, Lucas!" exclaims Catalina, alarmed.

"Oh, relax," answers her brother Lucas, who is leaning over the street with his arm inside the sewer. At that moment, a woman comes out of a store, sees them, and rushes over, concerned.

"Hey, you two! What are you doing?" she asks, alarmed.

"There's a kitten trapped in the sewer," explains Catalina. "We heard it when we were coming back from school, and my brother is trying to save it."

"Oh, no!" the woman gasps. "Poor thing!"

"I'm almost there," Lucas informs them, still focused on his task. "It's scared and won't let me grab it." "We should call the firefighters," suggests the woman, not knowing what to do.

"That won't work," says Lucas. "An adult's arm doesn't fit through here. Heck, not even mine fits! Catalina, your arm is smaller; you should try."

"Ew," exclaims Catalina. "The sewer is really dirty."

"Do you want to save the kitten or not?" her brother asks her.

Catalina sighs; indeed, the thought of that poor kitten trapped fills her with sadness. She is willing to do something as disgusting as putting her arm in that filthy sewer to save it. She can wash up at home later. And wash the kitten, too.

Determined, she kneels on the street beside her brother and inserts her arm. After a few moments, she feels the kitten's chest and tries to gently grab it. She has to proceed very slowly because she is afraid of hurting the poor thing, who is frightened and struggling.

Finally, when the kitten stops moving for a second, Catalina takes the chance and pulls her arm out of the sewer, along with a gray kitten.

"Oh, my goodness, it's adorable!" exclaims the woman. "Poor thing! We need to take it to the vet."

The children tell her that their mother is a veterinarian, so they will take the kitten home. Their mother can check it and make sure it's okay. So, after saying goodbye to the lady, Catalina and Lucas rush home with their little rescue.

Answer Key

—¡*Cuidado*, Lucas! —*exclama Catalina, asustada.*

—¡*Bah*! —*responde su hermano Lucas, que, recostado en la calle, tiene un brazo dentro de la alcantarilla.*

44

En ese momento, una mujer sale de una tienda, los ve y corre hacia ellos preocupada:

—¡Eh, ustedes dos! ¿Qué están haciendo? —quiere saber, alarmada.

—Hay un gatito atrapado en el alcantarillado —le explica Catalina—. Lo oímos cuando volvíamos de la escuela, y mi hermano está tratando de salvarlo.

—¡Oh, no! —se espanta la mujer—. ¡Pobrecito!

—Ya casi lo tengo —les avisa Lucas, todavía concentrado en su tarea—. Está asustado y no me deja sujetarlo. —Deberíamos llamar a los bomberos —sugiere la mujer, sin saber qué hacer.

—Eso no servirá —dice Lucas—. El brazo de un adulto no cabe por aquí. ¡Ay, ni siquiera el mío cabe! Catalina, tu brazo es más pequeño: deberías intentarlo tú.

—¡Puaj! —exclama Catalina—. La alcantarilla está muy sucia...

—¿Quieres salvar al gatito o no? —le pregunta su hermano.

Catalina suspira: en efecto, la idea de ese pobre gatito atrapado la llena de pena. Está dispuesta a hacer algo tan asqueroso como meter su brazo en esa sucia alcantarilla para salvarlo. Más tarde puede lavarse en casa. Y lavar al gatito, también.

Decidida, se arrodilla en la calle junto a su hermano y mete el brazo. Luego de unos momentos, siente el pecho del gatito e intenta sujetarlo con gentileza. Tiene que operar muy lentamente, teme hacerle daño al pobre bebé, que forcejea muy asustado.

Finalmente, en cuanto el gatito deja de moverse por un segundo, Catalina aprovecha la oportunidad y sube el brazo, que emerge de la alcantarilla con un gatito color gris.

—¡Oh, Dios mío: es precioso! —exclama la mujer, conmovida—. ¡Pobrecito! Hay que llevarlo al veterinario. Los niños le dicen que su madre es veterinaria, así que van a llevarlo a su casa. Su madre puede revisarlo y asegurarse de que está bien. Por lo tanto, luego de despedirse de la señora, Catalina y Lucas corren a casa junto al pequeño rescatado.

Key Takeaways

Good job! You have finished chapter 7, and you are getting closer to the finish line. In this chapter, you learned:

- What is an interjection?
- How to use them.
- And some English equivalents for Spanish interjections.

The next chapter is the last chapter of the first book! There, you will find some very useful tips to continue with your learning journey!

Chapter 8: Tips and Tricks

Tal vez nadie lo sepa... Como tal vez un día todos irán sabiendo lo que nadie sabía.
- José Ángel Buesa

Tips

Tip 1: "Tandem" is a very useful way to practice Spanish! There, you can talk with native Spanish speakers who can lend you a hand in your learning journey! Check it out at: https://www.tandem.net/practice/spanish.

Tip 2: To help you with your Spanish pronunciation, you can try this website, which will show you the approximate pronunciation of words: https://www.ingles.com/pronunciacion/hola. As you gain experience, you'll develop the ability to say new words out loud confidently.

Tip 3: Keep in mind that, in Spanish, you have to drop most pronouns. You will sound more natural and you will avoid misunderstandings.

Tip 4: Check out Oxford's free bilingual dictionary online at https://www.lexico.com/.

Tip 5: Watch movies in Spanish with Spanish subtitles on. You'll find it's a good way to improve your reading skills. After a while, try turning off the subtitles and writing down the words you hear. You can then check what you wrote with the subtitles.

Tip 6: In this first book, we've focused on the present indicative tense. Keep studying this tense until you feel comfortable with it before moving on to other verb tenses. Spanish has a lot of verb conjugations, which require time and patience, but don't be discouraged by this: you will get there in time. The imperative mood might be an exception to this tip, since it's easier than the rest. You can find an explanation here: https://grammar.collinsdictionary.com/es/gramatica-de-aprendizaje-espanol/the-imperative.

Tip 7: Look for someone who speaks Spanish to talk to! It can be a friend, a teacher, or someone who goes to your school. Having conversations with Spanish-speakers will definitely help you improve.

Tip 8: Don't be afraid to make mistakes. It's an important part of the learning process, and you won't improve without them.

Tip 9: Look for Spanish-speaking YouTubers and TikTokers and follow them! A lot of them speak both English and Spanish and share interesting information about the Spanish language and culture.

Effective Tricks

Trick 1: Identifying English words with Latin or French origins will make it easier to remember new vocabulary items, since both Spanish and French have their roots in Latin. English has been influenced by Latin and French, so there are many similar words.

Trick 2: When practicing speaking, do it slowly and with a steady pace. This gives you time to think and prevents you from stammering when you don't remember a word.

Trick 3: Remind the person you are talking to or the recipient of your text that you are a Spanish student. They will probably want to help you.

Trick 4: If you find yourself in front of a Spanish text that you don't understand, ask someone for their help, and don't rely on free translation tools. They can be misleading, and you might end up learning something that's wrong.

Trick 5: Gender awareness is important in Spanish-speaking cultures. This course follows the traditional approach to grammatical gender, which may be viewed as questionable or offensive by some people. Again, remind your conversation partner or reader that you are using the standard because you are a foreign learner and, if possible, ask them to explain their point of view. Even if you don't agree, it's important to stay informed about changes in the language you are learning.

Key Takeaways

¡Felicitaciones! This was the last chapter of Book 1 of **Complete Spanish for Middle & High School Students**. In this final chapter, we've seen:

- 9 tips to help you in your learning journey.
- 5 tricks to continue improving your Spanish.

Congratulations on reaching the end of Book 1! If you want to continue learning Spanish, don't hesitate to move on to our second book!

Conclusion

Learning a new language is indeed a rewarding journey, one that may span several years, but one that's worth embarking on. It demands dedication, persistence, and above all, love for knowledge!

As you've discovered throughout this book, a new language opens doors to a whole new culture... or even several new cultures, since Spanish is spoken in a lot of different countries across the globe! Our lessons have equipped you with the essential grammar skills of Spanish, and our stories have provided practice and have also offered a glimpse into the regular lives of some average Spanish speakers.

I hope this manual has guided you through the fundamental principles of Spanish grammar while also providing you with moments of enjoyment and cultural enrichment. Keep your enthusiasm alive and your curiosity burning. Continue your journey of learning, exploring, and connecting with the Spanish-speaking world. *¡Adelante y sigue aprendiendo!*

Book 2

Essential Spanish Vocabulary

Spanish Fundamentals

Introduction

Did you know that Spanish is not just a language but a vibrant tapestry of culture, heritage, and tradition? Here's a fascinating fact: there are over 40 million native Spanish speakers right here in the United States, making it a language that's not just spoken across the globe, but also in our own community.

In fact, more than 470 million people worldwide call Spanish their first language, making it the second most widely spoken language in the world in terms of native speakers. And guess what? Over 20 million people are actively learning Spanish as their second language, just like you!

But the benefits of learning Spanish go beyond impressive numbers. Whether you want to connect with family or friends who speak Spanish, study in a Spanish speaking country, travel for pleasure, or prepare for an exciting job opportunity, mastering Spanish will empower you to navigate a world of new experiences.

Essential Spanish Vocabulary is your trusty companion on this linguistic adventure. This book covers fundamental vocabulary and phrases from various aspects of life: from introducing yourself, traveling, and dining at a restaurant, to engaging in small talk, excelling at work, nurturing relationships, mastering shopping, and thriving in school.

You can begin by reading each chapter very closely. Rewriting some words and sentences will help you remember them. And don't forget to do the exercises at the end! Finally, remember to complement this book's vocabulary with the grammar lessons you had in the previous.

Are you ready to learn all the Spanish vocabulary you need to know to master the language? *¡Vamos!*

Chapter 1: *¿Quién eres?*

Soy un lector que escribe libros
- Arturo Pérez-Reverte

Introductions

Let's start by introducing ourselves. If you want to introduce yourself in Spanish, you say:

- *Me llamo...* ("My name is..."; literally: "I call myself...").
- *Soy...* ("I am...").

If you want to inquire about someone's name or identity, you say:

- *¿Cómo te llamas?* (Literally: "What do you call yourself?").
- *¿Cuál es tu nombre?* ("What's your name?").
- *¿Quién eres?* ("Who are you?").

If you want to be more formal about it, you should say:

- *¿Cómo se llama (usted)?* ("What's your name?").
- *¿Quién es (usted)?* ("Who are you?").

You should not forget that Spanish speakers have several words for "you," and each one has a different verb conjugation. That's why we say:

- Tú te llamas... ("Your name is..." informal).
- Usted se llama... ("Your name is..." formal).
- Ustedes se llaman... ("Your names are..." formal or informal, but plural. We use this one when speaking to more than one person).

To talk about your age, you say: A B C D E

- Tengo _____ años ("I am _____ years old").

This literally means "I have _____ years old," since that's the verb Spanish speakers use to talk about their age, as you learned in the previous book.

If you want to inquire about someone's age, you ask:

- *¿Cuántos años tienes?* ("How old are you?" Informal, the subject here is *tú*).
- *¿Cuántos años tiene?* ("How old are you?" Formal, the subject here is *usted*).

- *¿Cuántos años tienen?* ("How old are you?" Formal or informal, but plural; the subject here is *ustedes*).

These phrases literally mean "How many years do you have?"

If you want to talk about your origin or nationality, you say:

- *Soy de...* ("I am from..."). This expression is followed by the name of your country of origin.
- *Soy...* ("I am..."). This expression is followed by your nationality.

For example:

- *Soy de Chile* ("I am from Chile").
- *Soy chileno* ("I'm Chilean").

To inquire about someone's nationality, you can ask them:

- *¿De dónde eres (tú)?* ("Where are you from?" Informal).
- *¿De dónde es (usted)?* ("Where are you from?" Formal).
- *¿De dónde son (ustedes)?* ("Where are you from?" Formal or informal, but plural).

Now, here we have some phrases that Spanish speakers use when they meet someone for the first time:

- *Un placer.*
- *Un placer conocerte.*
- *Es un placer conocerte.*
- *Mucho gusto.*

They can all be translated as "Nice to meet you!"

Number 1-100

These are some basic cardinal numbers in Spanish:

SPANISH	ENGLISH
uno	one
dos	two
tres	three
cuatro	four
cinco	five
seis	six
siete	seven

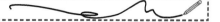

ocho	eight
nueve	nine
diez	ten
once	eleven
doce	twelve
trece	thirteen
catorce	fourteen
quince	fifteen
dieciséis	sixteen
diecisiete	seventeen
dieciocho	eighteen
diecinueve	nineteen
veinte	twenty
veintiuno	twentyone
veintidós	twentytwo
veintitrés	twentythree
veinticuatro	twentyfour
veinticinco	twentyfive
veintiséis	twentysix
veintisiete	twentyseven
veintiocho	twentyeight
veintinueve	twentynine
treinta	thirty
treinta y uno	thirtyone
treinta y dos	thirtytwo
cuarenta	fourty
cincuenta	fifty
sesenta	sixty
setenta	seventy
ochenta	eighty
noventa	ninety
cien	one hundred

You may also need to know the following numbers:

SPANISH	ENGLISH
doscientos	two hundred
trescientos	three hundred
cuatrocientos	four hundred
quinientos	five hundred
seiscientos	six hundred
setecientos	seven hundred
ochocientos	eight hundred
novecientos	nine hundred

Other important numbers are:

- *Mil* ("a thousand")
- *Un millón* ("a million")
- *Cero* ("zero")

Nationalities

The following nationalities correspond to most Spanish-speaking countries:

SPANISH	ENGLISH
argentino/a	Argentinean
boliviano/a	Bolivian
colombiano/a	Colombian
costarricense	Costa Rican
cubano/a	Cuban
dominicano/a	Dominican
español/a	Spanish
guatemalteco/a	Guatemalan
hondureño/a	Honduran
mexicano/a	Maxican
nicaragüense	Nicaraguan
paraguayo/a	Paraguayan

peruano/a	Preuvian
uruguayo/a	Uruguayan
venezolano/a	Venezuelan

Here you have some other demonyms, which correspond to other countries:

SPANISH	ENGLISH
estadounidense	American (from the United States)
chino/a	Chinese
japonés / japonesa	Japanese
francés / francesa	French
italiano/a	Italian
portugués / portuguesa	Portuguese
ruso/a	Russian
sudafricano	South African
australiano/a	Australian
coreano/a	Korean
alemán / alemana	German
inglés / inglesa	English
irlandés / irlandesa	Irish
ucraniano/a	Ukrainian
griego/a	Greek

Did you notice that, in the Spanish column, we have two words? That's because the first one is the one we use for men and the second one is the one we use for women.

Practice Time!

Read the following text and underline all the nationalities, countries, and ethnicities. Use the translation below to help you.

Cuando Austin entra a su primera clase universitaria, se da cuenta de que es temprano, pues el salón está vacío, a excepción de dos chicas que conversan entre sí.

Al sentarse, Austin se sorprende al notar que las chicas hablan en español. Él sabe un poco de ese idioma, así que se atreve a saludarlas y presentarse:

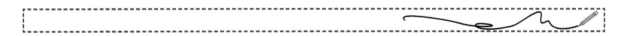

—*Hola. Soy Austin. ¿Ustedes cómo se llaman?*

—*¡Hola! —le contesta una de las chicas—. Mucho gusto. Soy Micaela y ella es Paola. ¿Hablas español?*

—*Un poquito —sonríe Austin —. Soy de Texas y tengo muchos amigos que hablan español. ¿Ustedes de dónde son?*

—*Yo soy argentina —se presenta Micaela—, pero mis padres son chinos. Me mudé sola a esta ciudad hace dos meses para ir a la universidad.*

—*Yo nací aquí, pero mi mamá es colombiana —comenta Paola.*

—*El esposo de mi tía es colombiano también —dice Austin—, pero mis primos no hablan mucho español.*

—*Es que yo viajo mucho a Colombia para visitar a mis abuelos —le explica Paola.*

—*Sí, yo también viajo a China cuando puedo para visitar a los míos —dice Micaela—. La primera vez que fui, tenía cuatro años.*

—*¿Cuántos años tienes? —pregunta Austin, pues es una pregunta que recuerda de sus clases de español.*

—*Tengo dieciocho. ¿Y tú?*

—*Yo tengo diecinueve.*

—*¿Hay muchos inmigrantes chinos en Argentina?*

—*¡Oh, sí! Muchísimos. Argentina tiene una comunidad asiática oriental muy grande. A los latinos, además, nos gusta mucho la cultura asiática.*
En ese momento, un hombre barbudo se asoma a la puerta y los tres hacen silencio, pues comprenden que el profesor ha llegado.

Ⓐ Translation

When Austin walks into his first college lesson, he realizes he is early because the classroom is empty, except for two girls who are chatting.

As he takes his seat, Austin is surprised to notice that the girls are speaking in Spanish. He knows a bit of that language, so he dares to greet them and introduce himself:

"Hello. I'm Austin. What are your names?"

"Hello!" replies one of the girls. "Nice to meet you. I'm Micaela, and she's Paola. Do you speak Spanish?"

"A little," replies Austin with a smile. "I'm from Texas, and I have many friends who speak Spanish.

Where are you girls from?"

"I'm Argentinian," says Micaela, introducing herself, "but my parents are Chinese. I moved to this city by myself two months ago to go to college."

"I was born here, but my mom is Colombian," says Paola.

"My aunt's husband is Colombian too," says Austin, "but my cousins don't speak much Spanish."

"I travel to Colombia often to visit my grandparents," explains Paola.

"Yes, I also travel to China when I can to visit mine,"adds Micaela. "The first time I went, I was four years old."

"How old are you?" Austin asks her, since it is one of the questions he remembers from his Spanish lessons.

"I'm eighteen. And you?"

"I'm nineteen."

"Are there many Chinese immigrants in Argentina?"

"Oh, yes! A lot. Argentina has a very large East Asian community. Besides, Latin people really enjoy Asian culture."

At that moment, a bearded man appears at the door, and the three of them become silent because they understand that the professor has arrived.

✓ Answer Key

Cuando Austin entra a su primera clase universitaria, se da cuenta de que es temprano, pues el salón está vacío, a excepción de dos chicas que conversan entre sí.

Al sentarse, Austin se sorprende al notar que las chicas hablan en español. Él sabe un poco de ese idioma, así que se atreve a saludarlas y presentarse:

—Hola. Soy Austin. ¿Ustedes cómo se llaman?

—¡Hola! —le contesta una de las chicas—. Mucho gusto. Soy Micaela y ella es Paola. ¿Hablas español?

—Un poquito —sonríe Austin —. Soy de Texas y tengo muchos amigos que hablan español. ¿Ustedes de dónde son?

—Yo soy <u>argentina</u> —se presenta Micaela—, pero mis padres son chinos. Me mudé sola a esta ciudad hace dos meses para ir a la universidad.

—*Yo nací aquí, pero mi mamá es* <u>*colombiana*</u> —*comenta Paola.*

—*El esposo de mi tía es* <u>*colombiano*</u> *también* —*dice Austin*—*, pero mis primos no hablan mucho español.*

—*Es que yo viajo mucho a* <u>*Colombia*</u> *para visitar a mis abuelos* —*le explica Paola.*

—*Sí, yo también viajo a* <u>*China*</u> *cuando puedo para visitar a los míos* —*dice Micaela*—*. La primera vez que fui, tenía cuatro años.*

—*¿Cuántos años tienes?* —*pregunta Austin, pues es una pregunta que recuerda de sus clases de español.*

—*Tengo dieciocho. ¿Y tú?*

—*Yo tengo diecinueve.*

—*¿Hay muchos inmigrantes* <u>*chinos*</u> *en* <u>*Argentina*</u>?

—*¡Oh, sí! Muchísimos.* <u>*Argentina*</u> *tiene una comunidad* <u>*asiática oriental*</u> *muy grande. A los* <u>*latinos*</u>*, además, nos gusta mucho la cultura* <u>*asiática*</u>.

En ese momento, un hombre barbudo se asoma a la puerta y los tres hacen silencio, pues comprenden que el profesor ha llegado.

Practice a Bit More!

Now it's your turn to introduce yourself! Write a short text with your name, age and nationality. For example:

Me llamo Chelsea, tengo quince años y soy estadounidense.

Key Takeaways

Congratulations on finishing chapter 1! In this first chapter, you've learned a lot of new vocabulary:

- All the words and expressions to introduce yourself and to ask about someone's identity and personal information.
- The most important numbers in Spanish.
- The names of Spanish-speaking and other nationalities.

Now that you know how to introduce yourself, say your and and nationality, are you ready for the next step? Chapter 2 will teach you how to navigate small talk and normal conversations!

Chapter 2: *Small Talk and Normal Conversations*

Cuando se encapota el sol en jueves, antes del domingo llueve.
- Popular saying

This chapter will provide you with some very useful vocabulary you will probably find yourself needing a lot in any given conversation! We'll cover the days of the week, the months of the year, the colors and much more!

The Days of the Week

Let's begin with *los días de la semana* ("the days of the week"). Did you know that a bunch of them are named after ancient Roman deities? Two other things you need to know: in Spanish, the days of the week are not capitalized. Also, they are all masculine words. Now yes, let's check them out:

SPANISH	ENGLISH
lunes	Monday
martes	Tuesday
miércoles	Wednesday
jueves	Thursday
viernes	Friday
sábado	Saturday
domingo	Sunday

The Months of the Year

To be able to say what day it is today, you'll also need to know *los meses del año* ("the months of the year"). Note that the months of the year are also written in lowercase.

SPANISH	ENGLISH
enero	January
febrero	February
marzo	March
abril	April

mayo	May
junio	June
julio	July
agosto	August
septiembre	September
octubre	October
noviembre	November
diciembre	December

The Date in Spanish

Now you know the days of the week and the months of the year in Spanish, you are ready to say the date. Follow this structure:

- *Hoy es miércoles 13 de septiembre* ("Today is Wednesday, September 13").

Now complete the following sentence with today's date!

- *Hoy es_____ ___ de_____.*

More Vocabulary to Talk about Dates

Lastly, this extra vocabulary is also important to talk about dates and the calendar:

SPANISH	ENGLISH
mañana	tomorrow
ayer	yesterday
tarde	late
temprano	early
semana	week
día	day
mes	month
año	year
verano	summer
otoño	fall
invierno	winter

| primavera | spring |

The Colors

Now, *los colores* ("the colors")! As nouns, they are all masculine words. As adjectives, some of them change in gender and all of them change in number.

SPANISH	ENGLISH
rojo/a	red
verde	green
azul	blue
negro/a	black
blanco/a	white
marrón	brown
rosa	pink
naranja	orange
amarillo/a	yellow
violeta	violet
gris	grey
celeste	light blue

Colors are important words in any language. You'll find yourself using them to describe a wide variety of things, so you better study them!

The Parts of the Body

It's time to learn the names of *las partes del cuerpo* ("the parts of the body"). In this list, we'll add the article before each noun, to let you know whether the words are masculine or feminine.

SPANISH	ENGLISH
la cabeza	head
el pelo / el cabello	hair
la cara / el rostro	face
el ojo	eye

la nariz	nose
la boca	mouth
el labio	lip
el diente	tooth
la lengua	tongue
la oreja	ear
el cuello	neck
el hombro	shoulder
el brazo	arm
el pecho	chest
la mano	hand
el dedo	finger
la espalda	back
el estómago	stomach
la pierna	leg
la rodilla	knee
el pie	foot
la piel	skin
el codo	elbow
la uña	nail

With all of this new vocabulary you are ready to embark in a lot of conversations!

Practice Time!

Read the following text:

Después del colegio, en el autobús, Mariana y Luz conversan:

—¡Qué cansada estoy! —exclama Mariana.

—Yo también —suspira Luz—. Y recién es miércoles... ¡Ojalá fuera viernes!

—¡Ojalá! Este fin de semana, mi mamá va a llevarme de compras por mi cumpleaños.

—Pero tu cumpleaños es en octubre...

—*Ya lo sé, pero es que hay algo que quiero comprar.*

—*¿Qué quieres comprar?*

—*Hay una nueva crema para acné que quiero probar. No recuerdo cómo se llama, pero viene en un envase violeta.*

—*Sí, creo que sé cuál es. Pero no sé si deberías usar esa crema en este momento del año.*

—*¿Y cuándo debería usarla?*

—*En diciembre, probablemente. Es una crema para el invierno, cuando hay poco sol.*

—*¿Cómo sabes eso?*

—*Una TikToker que sigo la usa y tiene muy linda piel. Pero dice que hay que usarla en invierno, no en verano.*

—*¿Qué TikToker?*

—*Alavasia.*

—*¡¿En serio?! ¡Me encanta Alavasia! Tiene una piel muy linda y un cabello increíble.*

—*Sí, es mi favorita.*

Ⓐ Translation

Now, read the translation:

After school, on the bus, Mariana and Luz are talking:

"I'm so tired!" exclaims Mariana.

"Me too," says Luz, sighing, "and it's only Wednesday... I wish it were Friday!"

"Me too! This weekend, my mom is taking me shopping for my birthday."

"But your birthday is in October..."

"I know, but there's something I want to get."

"What do you want to get?"

"There's a new acne cream I want to try. I don't remember the name, but it comes in a purple package."

"Yeah, I think I know which one you mean. But I don't know if you should use that cream right now."

"And when should I use it?"

"Probably in December. It's a winter cream, for when there's not much sun."

"How do you know that?"

"A TikToker I follow uses it and has really nice skin. But she says you should use it during winter, not in the summer."

"Which TikToker?"

"Alavasia."

"Really?! I love Alavasia! She has beautiful skin and amazing hair."

"Yes, she's my favorite."

 Practice!

Now, read the text again and fill in the blanks. However, this time you don't have to use the same words as in the original text. Use the vocabulary you have learned in this chapter to complete the text in a way that still makes sense.

Después del colegio, en el autobús, Mariana y Luz conversan:

—¡Qué cansada estoy! —exclama Mariana.

—Yo también —suspira Luz—. Y recién es _____ ... ¡Ojalá fuera _____ !

—¡Ojalá! Este fin de semana, mi mamá va a llevarme de compras por mi cumpleaños.

—Pero tu cumpleaños es en _____ ...

—Ya lo sé, pero es que hay algo que quiero comprar.

—¿Qué quieres comprar?

—Hay una nueva crema para acné que quiero probar. No recuerdo cómo se llama, pero viene en un envase _____ .

—Sí, creo que sé cuál es. Pero no sé si deberías usar esa crema en este momento del año.

—¿Y cuándo debería usarla?

—En _____, probablemente. Es una crema para el invierno, cuando hay poco sol.

—¿Cómo sabes eso?

—Una TikToker que sigo la usa y tiene muy linda piel. Pero dice que hay que usarla en invierno, no en verano.

—¿Qué TikToker?

—Alavasia.

—¡¿En serio?! ¡Me encanta Alavasia! Tiene una _____ muy linda y un _____ increíble.

—Sí, es mi favorita.

Key Takeaways

You have reached the end of chapter 2, good job! In this chapter you've learned a lot of new vocabulary.

- The days of the week.
- The months of the year.
- How to say the date.
- Some extra vocabulary.
- The colors.
- The parts of the human body.

If you are planning a trip to a Spanish-speaking country, you shouldn't miss our next chapter, where we'll be talking about traveling!

Chapter 3: Addresses and Travels

Viajar es imprescindible y la sed de viaje es un síntoma neto de inteligencia.
- Enrique Jardiel Poncela

Asking for Directions

As young students, you might not have had many opportunities to explore new places by yourselves. However, there will come a time when you'll need to ask for directions, whether you're going to a friend's house, traveling to a new city, or simply navigating an unfamiliar part of town. Learning how to ask for directions in Spanish is an essential skill to have in your linguistic toolkit!

💬 Polite Phrases

When approaching someone to ask for directions, it's polite to use an expressions such as:

- *Por favor* ("please")
- *Disculpa / perdona* ("excuse me," informal)
- *Disculpe / perdone* ("excuse me," formal)

For instance, you can say:

- *Perdona, ¿puedes ayudarme?* ("Excuse me, can you help me?" Informal).
- *Disculpe, ¿puede ayudarme?* ("Excuse me, can you help me?" Formal).

💬 Asking Where a Place Is

After the polite expression to address someone, you can say: *¿Dónde está...?* ("Where is...?"), followed by the place or location you're looking for. For example:

- *¿Dónde está la estación de tren?* ("Where is the train station?").

If the place you want to go to is a plural noun, you have to say: *¿Dónde están...?* ("Where are...?"), followed by the place. For example:

- *¿Dónde están las paradas de autobús?* ("Where are the bus stops?").

Another question you may ask is *¿Cómo llego a...?* ("How do I get to...?"), followed by the place you're looking for. For example:

- *¿Cómo llego a la playa?* ("How do I get to the beach?").

💬 Orienting Yourself:

It's a good idea to mention a nearby landmark or street to provide context for your question. You can say: *Estoy cerca de...* ("I am near...") or *En la esquina de...* ("On the corner of..."). For instance:

- *Estoy cerca de la plaza principal* ("I am near the main square").

Understanding Directions

When someone gives you directions, listen carefully and feel free to ask them to repeat or clarify if needed.

Common directional phrases include:

- *Derecha* ("right")
- *Izquierda* ("left")
- *Recto / derecho* ("straight")
- *Girar* ("turn")
- *Esquina* ("corner")
- *Calle* ("street")

For example:

- *Gira a la derecha en la segunda calle* ("Turn right on the second street").

💬 Expressing Gratitude

After receiving directions, you are going to want to thank the person who helped you. You can say:

- *Gracias* ("Thank you").
- *Gracias por tu ayuda* ("Thank you for your help," informal).
- *Gracias por su ayuda* ("Thank you for your help," formal).

Addresses

It's also important to know how to say an address (*dirección*) in Spanish. This can vary from place to place, but the usual way is:

The name of the street:

- *Calle Ecuador* ("Ecuador Street")
- *Avenida Corrientes* ("Corrientes Avenue")

The number:

- *Avenida Corrientes 1789* ("1789 Corrientes Avenue")

The floor and apartament:

- *Avenida Corrientes 1789, piso 10, apartamento B* ("1789 Corrientes Avenue, apartment 10 B")

At the end, you can add the city, province and country, as well as the zip code.

- *Ciudad* ("city")
- *Provincia / estado* ("province / state")
- *País* ("country")
- *Código postal* ("zip code")

At the Restaurant

Let's begin with some essential food vocabulary:

SPANISH	ENGLISH	SPANISH	ENGLISH
la fruta	fruit	*la verdura / el vegetal*	vegetable
la manzana	apple	*la banana/ el plátano*	banana
la zanahoria	carrot	*el tomate*	tomato
la uva	grape	*la papa / la patata*	potato
la cebolla	onion	*el pepino*	cucumber
el pepinillo	pickle	*la carne*	meat
el pollo	chicken	*el pescado*	fish
el pan	bread	*el queso*	cheese
la leche	milk	*el huevo*	egg
el cereal	cereal	*la sal*	salt
el azúcar	sugar	*la sopa*	soup
el helado	ice cream	*el pastel*	cake
el chocolate	chocolate	*el café*	coffee
el té	tea	*el jugo*	juice
el agua	water	*el vino*	wine
la cerveza	beer	*la galleta*	cookie
la almendra	almond	*la nuez*	nut
el coco	coconut	*la hamburguesa*	hamburguer
el maní	peanut	*la fresa*	strawberry
la cereza	cherry	*el arándano*	blueberry

la avena	oatmeal	*la lechuga*	lettuce
el ajo	garlic	*el jamón*	ham
la salchicha	sausage	*la mermelada*	jam
la mantequilla / la manteca	butter	*las papas fritas*	French fries
el caramelo	caramel	*la canela*	cinnamon
la pimienta	pepper	*el arroz*	rice
la harina	flour	*el maíz*	corn
el trigo	wheat		

Studying the Menu

Now you know some vocabulary about food in Spanish, you can study the menu. Common menu terms to know include:

- *Entradas* ("appetizers")
- *Platos principales* ("main courses")
- *Bebidas* ("beverages")
- *Postres* ("desserts")
- *Plato del día* ("dish of the day")

Once you are ready, *un mesero* ("waiter") or *una mesera* ("waitress") will come to take your order.

💬 Ordering Drinks

Start by ordering drinks. You can say: *Para beber, quisiera...* ("To drink, I would like...") followed by your choice. For instance:

- *Para beber, quisiera un refresco* ("To drink, I would like a soda").
- *Para beber, quisiera un vaso de agua mineral* ("To drink, I would like a glass of mineral water").

💬 Placing Your Order

To order your food, you can use phrases like: *Me gustaría...* ("I would like...") or *Quisiera...* ("I would like..."), followed by the name of the dish. If you have specific preferences or modifications, kindly communicate them. Finish with *por favor*. For example:

- *Me gustaría el filete bien cocido, por favor* ("I would like the steak well-done, please").

Special Dietary Requests

If you have dietary restrictions or allergies, make sure you tell the server about them. Phrases like *Soy alérgico/a a...* ("I'm allergic to...") are essential for your safety.

Expressing Quantity

Use numbers to specify the amount of items you want. For example:

- *Dos tacos de pollo* ("Two chicken tacos")
- *Una ensalada grande* ("One large salad")
- *Tres porciones de pizza* ("Three pizza slices")

Asking for Recommendations

If you're unsure about what to order, you can ask the server: *¿Qué me recomienda?* ("What do you recommend?").

They may suggest popular or signature dishes.

Courtesy and Gratitude

Be polite and show appreciation. Say *Gracias* ("thank you") when receiving your food or drinks.

Payment and Tipping

In some countries, the bill may be brought to your table when you're ready to leave. You can ask for it by saying: *La cuenta, por favor* ("The bill, please").

Tipping practices vary by country, so it's a good idea to inquire or check local customs. "The tip" is *la propina*.

Enjoy your Meal

Once your food arrives, you can wish your companions *¡Buen provecho!*, which means "enjoy your meal!," before you start eating.

At the Airport

If you're traveling to a Spanish-speaking country, you will also need some airport related vocabulary. These are some of the words you'll probably encounter:

Checking In

- *Pase de abordar* ("Boarding Pass")
- *Boleto de avión* ("Flight Ticket")
- *Pasaporte* ("Passport")
- *Equipaje* ("Luggage")
- *Control de seguridad* ("Security Check")

At the Terminal

- *Puerta de embarque* ("Boarding gate")
- *Salidas* ("Departures")
- *Llegadas* ("Arrivals")
- *Sala de espera* ("Airport lounge")
- *Vuelo retrasado* ("Delayed flight")
- *Anuncio* ("Announcement")

On the Plane

- *Asiento* ("Seat")
- *Pasillo* ("Aisle")
- *Ventana* ("Window")
- *Cinturón de seguridad* ("Seat belt")
- *Auxiliar de vuelo* ("Flight attendant")

During the Flight

- *Comida a bordo* ("In-flight meal")
- *Carrito de bebidas* ("Beverage cart")
- *Compartimento superior* ("Overhead compartment")
- *Baño* ("Restroom")
- *Turbulencia* ("Turbulence")

Arrival

- *Aduanas* ("Customs")
- *Migraciones* ("Immigration")
- *Cinta transportadora de equipaje* ("Baggage carousel")
- *Transporte del aeropuerto* ("Airport shuttle")
- *Zona de recogida* ("Pick-up area")

💬 Some Useful Phrases

- *¿Dónde está la puerta para el vuelo...?* ("Where is the gate for flight...?").
- *Necesito facturar mi equipaje* ("I need to check my luggage").
- *¿A qué hora sale/llega el vuelo...?* ("What time does the flight... depart/arrive?").
- *¿Hay un transporte al centro de la ciudad?* ("Is there a shuttle to the city center?").

Numbers and Time

- *Número de vuelo* ("Flight number")
- *Hora de salida* ("Departure time")
- *Hora de llegada* ("Arrival time")
- *Número de puerta* ("Gate number")
- *Número de terminal* ("Terminal number")
- *Mostrador* ("Counter")

Emergency

- *Salida de emergencia* ("Emergency exit")
- *Chaleco salvavidas* ("Life vest")
- *Evacuación de emergencia* ("Emergency evacuation")
- *Aterrizaje de emergencia* ("Emergency landing")

Learning these airport-related words and phrases in Spanish will help you navigate the airport with confidence and ensure a smoother travel experience!

Practice Time!

Match these words in Spanish with their equivalent terms in English.

SPANISH	ENGLISH
calle	juice
manzana	lettuce
vino	French fries
avenida	cheese
boleto	jam
queso	fruit
lechuga	seat
cebolla	milk
bebida	avenue
papas fritas	wine
llegada	onion
asiento	ticket
equipaje	beverage
mermelada	apple
leche	street
jugo	luggage
fruta	arrival

Now, translate the following English words into Spanish.

ENGLISH	SPANISH
left	
right	
gate	
bill	
dessert	
seat belt	
allergic	
salad	
appetizer	
waiter	

⊘ Answer Key

SPANISH	ENGLISH
calle	juice
manzana	lettuce
vino	French fries
avenida	cheese
boleto	jam
queso	fruit
lechuga	seat
cebolla	milk
bebida	avenue
papas fritas	wine
llegada	onion
asiento	ticket
equipaje	beverage
mermelada	apple
leche	street
jugo	luggage
fruta	arrival

ENGLISH	SPANISH
left	izquierda
right	derecha

gate	*puerta*
bill	*cuenta*
dessert	*postre*
seat belt	*cinturón de seguridad*
allergic	*alérgico*
salad	*ensalada*
appetizer	*entrada*
waiter	*mesero*

 Practice a Bit More!

Read the following short story. Pay special attention to the vocabulary you've just learned and to the new words you'll find.

Luego de tres escalas y diecisiete horas de viaje, están en Madrid. Tras dejar el equipaje en el hotel, Rachel y su madre están hambrientas y deciden buscar un restaurante en donde cenar.

Como Rachel habla español mejor que su madre, es ella quien se acerca a un transeúnte para preguntarle en dónde puede encontrar un buen restaurante.

——¡Ah, sí! ——exclama el hombre——. Hay varios por aquí. ¿Pero vosotras qué queréis? ¿Tapas? ¿O una comida más abundante?

Rachel titubea, sin entender una sola palabra. ¿Qué quiere decir "vosotras"? ¿"Queréis"? ¿Y "tapas"?

*——Si queréis ir de tapas, hay un lugar muy chulo del otro lado de la plaza. Pero no vayáis al de la esquina,
que ese es bien cutre... Ah, pero, para comer algo tradicional español, id a aquel lugar que veis allá a la derecha, que preparan una paella que uno flipa...*

Rachel ya perdió la cuenta de todas las palabras que no comprende, de modo que, avergonzada, le da las gracias al hombre y vuelve junto a su madre. No tiene idea de por qué le fue tan difícil entender al desconocido, ya que le va muy bien en español.

Finalmente, deciden preguntar en la recepción del hotel, en donde les recomiendan un restaurante y les explican qué son las tapas.

Unos días después, Rachel ya sabe que en España se dice "vosotros" en lugar de "ustedes" y que los verbos se conjugan de manera diferente. Además, ya está familiarizada con muchas palabras de la jerga local que no enseñan en la escuela.

En la última noche de las vacaciones, Rachel ya sabe cómo ordenar en el restaurante:

——Por favor, queremos unas tapas para empezar. Luego, una ensalada de zanahoria y lechuga para mi madre. Y yo quisiera pescado con huevo frito. De postre, quiero el helado con salsa de chocolate.

Rachel se detiene cuando ve que su madre le señala algo detrás de ella. Voltea para descubrir que, en la mesa de al lado, está sentado el caballero a quien le pidió direcciones el primer día. Él las reconoce y las dos lo saludan.
Rachel se siente enormemente satisfecha de entender todo lo que el hombre le dice.

Ⓐ Translation

After three layovers and seventeen hours of travel, they are in Madrid. After leaving their luggage at the hotel, Rachel and her mother are hungry and decide to find a restaurant to have dinner.

Since Rachel speaks Spanish better than her mother, she is the one who approaches a passerby to ask where they can find a good restaurant.

"Oh, yes!" exclaims the man. "There are several around here. But what do you want? Tapas? Or a bigger meal?"

Rachel hesitates, not understanding a single word. What did he mean by "vosotras"? "Queréis"? And "tapas"?

"If you want tapas, there's a really cool place on the other side of the square. But don't go to the one on the corner; that one is pretty lousy... Oh, but if you want to have a traditional Spanish meal, go to that place over there on the right; they make a paella that's out of this world..."

Rachel loses count of all the words she can't understand, so she thanks the man and returns to her mother, feeling embarrassed. She has no idea why she found it so difficult to understand the stranger; she does well in Spanish.

Finally, they decide to ask at the hotel's front desk, where they recommend a restaurant and explain to them what tapas are.

A few days later, Rachel already knows that in Spain they use "vosotros" instead of "ustedes" and that verbs are conjugated differently. Besides, she's already familiar with many local slang words that are not taught at school.

On the last night of their holiday, Rachel knows how to order in the restaurant:

"Please, we'd like some tapas to start. Then, a carrot and lettuce salad for my mother. And I would like fish with fried eggs. For dessert, I want an ice cream with chocolate sauce."

Rachel stops when she sees her mother is pointing something behind her. She turns around to discover that the man she asked for directions on the first day is sitting at the table next to them. He recognizes them, and they both greet him. Rachel feels immensely satisfied because she can understand everything the man is saying.

Key Takeaways

Congratulations on your hard work! You are done with chapter 3, which has thought you several new things:

- How to tell an address in Spanish.
- How to ask for directions.
- How to order food at a restaurant.
- A lot of food vocabulary.
- Important airport related vocabulary.

After this travel-related chapter, it's time to go back home! In Chapter 4, we'll talk about the household and we'll have some fun talking about shopping!

Chapter 4: Household and Shopping

Siempre imaginé que el Paraíso sería algún tipo de biblioteca.
- Jorge Luis Borges

In this chapter, we will explore essential vocabulary related to the home. Then, we'll learn some important shopping-related words.

Home sweet home

Let's begin with some household items.

SPANISH	ENGLISH
la computadora	computer
el teclado	keyboard
el celular	cellphone
la silla	chair
la mesa	table
la cama	bed
el escritorio	desk
el refrigerador	refrigerator
la manta	blanket
el vaso	glass
el plato	plate
el tenedor	fork
el cuchillo	knife
la cortina	curtain
el armario	closet
el horno	oven
la lavadora	washing machine
la taza	mug
el fregadero / lavabo	sink

el inodoro	toilet
la ducha	shower
la televisión	television
los muebles	forniture
el sofá	sofa

Next, let's learn about the different parts of the house!

SPANISH	ENGLISH
el cuarto / la habitación	room
la cocina	kitchen
el baño	bathroom
el pasillo	corridor
el recibidor	hall
el balcón	balcony
el jardín	garden
el patio	patio
la habitación de huéspedes	guest room
el comedor	dining room
la sala	living room
el sótano	basement
el ático	attic
la biblioteca	library

Practice Time!

First, read the following description and its translation.

La casa de mis abuelos es mi lugar favorito. Es antigua y tiene un jardín muy grande. Las habitaciones son amplias y los muebles son muy hermosos, porque mis abuelos aman la decoración. Además, todos los cuartos son luminosos y los techos son altos.

La casa tiene cuatro habitaciones. La habitación de mis abuelos es la más grande. Las paredes son blancas, como las cortinas. Hay un mueble de madera muy antiguo que mi abuela dice que perteneció a su propia abuela.

78

La sala tiene tres sillones y un televisor, aunque a mis abuelos no les gusta mirar televisión. Prefieren pasar el tiempo en el jardín, jugando tenis o cuidando las plantas.

Lo más curioso de la casa es el sótano. Es enorme, oscuro y misterioso. Mi hermano y yo a veces bajamos a explorarlo y encontramos cajas viejas con fotos de nuestra mamá cuando era pequeña.

Nosotros, en cambio, vivimos en un departamento. Mi habitación es azul, pero las cortinas son color beige. Tengo un escritorio con mi computadora, una cama y un armario blanco en donde guardo mi ropa y otras cosas. También tengo una batería. Además, en un rincón, está la cama de mi perro Pumba.

A. Translation

My grandparents' house is my favorite place. It's old and has a very large garden. The rooms are spacious, and the furniture is beautiful because my grandparents love decoration. Moreover, all the rooms are bright, and the ceilings are high.

The house has four bedrooms. My grandparents' bedroom is the largest. The walls are white, just like the curtains. There's a very old wooden piece of furniture that my grandmother says belonged to her own grandmother.

The living room has three armchairs and a television, although my grandparents don't like watching TV. They prefer spending their time in the garden, playing tennis, or taking care of the plants.

The most intriguing part of the house is the basement. It's huge, dark, and mysterious. My brother and I sometimes go down to explore it and find old boxes with photos of our mom when she was a child.

We, on the other hand, live in an apartment. My room is blue, but the curtains are beige. I have a desk with my computer, a bed, and a white wardrobe where I keep my clothes and other things. I also have a drum kit. Additionally, in one corner, there's my dog Pumba's bed.

Now, write your own description of your house! Use the following sentences:

- *Vivo en una casa/apartamento* ("I live in a house / apartment")
- *Mi casa/apartamento es...* ("My house/apartment is...")
- *Mi cuarto es...* ("My room is...")
- *Tengo...* ("I have...")
- *Hay...* ("There is / there are...")

Your description:

_____

_____

_____

_____

_____

_____

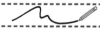
Going Shopping

When we go shopping, it's very common to use demonstrative pronouns or adjectives, such as...

- *Este/a* ("This one")
- *Ese/a* ("That one")
- *Estos/as* ("These ones")
- *Esos/as* ("Those ones")

Remember: we use the ones ending in A for female nouns and the ones ending in E or O for masculines ones.

Now, let's dive into some basic shopping vocabulary!

Grocery Shopping

- *Supermercado* (" Supermarket")
- *Lista de compras* ("Shopping list")
- *Carrito de compras* ("Shopping cart")
- *Caja registradora* ("Cash register")
- *Pago digital* ("Digital payment")
- *Comprar* ("To buy")
- *Vendedor/a* ("Salesperson")
- *Precio* ("Price")
- *Gasto* ("Expense")
- *Regatear* ("To haggle")
- *Cliente* ("Customer")
- *Cambio* ("Money exchange ")
- *Recibo* ("Receipt")

Useful Sentences:

- *Necesito hacer compras* ("I need to go shopping").
- *¿Dónde está el supermercado más cercano?* ("Where is the nearest supermarket?").
- *¿Tienen pan fresco?* ("Do you have fresh bread?").
- *¿Cuánto cuesta esto?* ("How much does this cost?").
- *¿Aceptan tarjetas de crédito/débito?* ("Do you accept credit/debit cards?").
- *Necesito pagar en efectivo* ("I need to pay in cash").
- *Este artículo está en oferta* ("This item is on sale").

Also, don't forget that different countries have different payment apps! It may be a good idea to do a bit of research about digital payment apps when visiting a new country.

Shopping for Clothes

- *Ropa* ("Clothing")
- *Tienda de ropa* ("Clothing store")

- *Camisa* ("Shirt")
- *Pantalones* ("Pants")
- *Vestido* ("Dress")
- *Zapatos* ("Shoes")
- *Talla* ("Size")
- *Color* ("Color")
- *Probador* ("Fitting room")
- *Oferta* ("Sale")
- *Descuento* ("Discount")

💬 Useful Sentences:

- *¿Tienen esta camisa en una talla más grande/pequeña?* ("Do you have this shirt in a larger/smaller size?").
- *Me gusta el vestido azul* ("I like the blue dress").
- *¿Puedo probarme estos zapatos?* ("Can I try on these shoes?").
- *¿Cuánto cuesta con el descuento?* ("How much does it cost with the discount?").
- *No es mi talla* ("It's not my size").
- *Este vestido no combina con este sombrero* ("This dress doesn't match this hat").
- *¿Tiene esto en otro color?* ("Do you have this in another color?").
- *Estoy mirando* ("I'm just looking").

Practice Time!

Read the following text:

Andrés y su padre están comprando zapatos. Llevan casi dos horas en la tienda, y Andrés se siente extremadamente cansado. No entiende por qué su padre no puede simplemente comprarle un par de zapatos. Para él, todos se ven iguales.

—Estos me gustan —dice Andrés, señalando los zapatos que se está probando.

—No estoy seguro —duda su padre—. Se ven pequeños...

—No son pequeños: se sienten bien —insiste Andrés.

—Ahora se sienten bien, pero en unos meses crecerás y ya no te quedarán.

—Bueno, entonces compremos una talla más grande.

—Pero dijiste que esos te quedaban demasiado sueltos.

—¡Mentí! Compremos estos y vámonos a comer.

—Andrés, esto es importante.

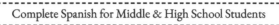

—*¿Por qué no te pruebas estos zapatos deportivos?* —*le sugiere la vendedora*—. *Están en oferta. Además, incluyen una gorra de regalo.*

—*¿Los tienes en otro color?*

—*Los tenemos en negro, blanco y azul.*

—*Bueno, tráelos todos para que mi hijo se los pruebe. ¿Qué hay de esos zapatos de allá? ¿Esos tienen algún descuento?*

—*Voy a preguntar* —*dice la vendedora, y se dirige al mostrador.*

Andrés suspira. Se da cuenta de que no se irán de la tienda pronto.

(A) Translation

Now, read the translation:

Andrés and his father are buying shoes. They have been in the store for nearly two hours, and Andrés feels extremely tired. He doesn't understand why his father can't just buy him a pair of shoes. They all look the same to him.

"I like these," he says, pointing to the shoes he is trying on.

"I'm not sure," says his father, hesitating. "They look small..."

"They're not small; they feel good," insists Andrés.

"They may feel good now, but in a few months, you'll grow, and they won't fit anymore."

"Well, then let's buy a larger size."

"But you said those were too loose."

"I lied! Let's just buy those and go to eat."

"Andrés, this is important."

"Why don't you try these sneakers?" suggests the shop attendant. "They are on sale and come with a free cap."

"Do you have them in another color?"

"We have them in black, white, and blue."

"Well, bring them all so my son can try them on. What about those shoes over there? Do they have

any discounts?"

"I'll check," says the shop attendant, and goes to the counter.

Andrés sighs. He realizes they wouldn't be leaving the store anytime soon.

 Practice!

Now read the text again, but this time Andrés and his father are buying a T-shirt instead of shoes. Fill in the blanks with the correct words:

Andrés y su padre están comprando _____. Llevan casi dos horas en la tienda, y Andrés se siente extremadamente cansado. No entiende por qué su padre no puede simplemente comprarle cualquier camiseta. Para él, _____ se ven iguales.

—_____ me gustan —dice Andrés, señalando _____ que se está probando.

—No estoy seguro —duda su padre—. Se ve _____...

—No es _____: se siente bien —insiste Andrés.

—Ahora se siente bien, pero en unos meses crecerás y ya no te quedará.

—Bueno, entonces compremos una talla más grande.

—Pero dijiste que _____ te quedaban demasiado _____.

—¡Mentí! Compremos _____ y vámonos a comer.

—Andrés, esto es importante.

—¿Por qué no te pruebas esta camiseta? —le sugiere la vendedora—. Está en oferta. Además, incluyen una gorra de regalo.

—¿_____ tienes en otro color?

—_____ tenemos en negro, blanco y azul.

—Bueno, tráelas todas para que mi hijo se las pruebe. ¿Qué hay de _____ de allá? ¿_____ tienen algún descuento?

—Voy a preguntar —dice la vendedora, y se dirige al mostrador.
Andrés suspira. Se da cuenta de que no se irán de la tienda pronto.

✓ **Answer Key**

una camiseta; todas; esta; la (camiseta); pequeña; pequeña; esa; suelta; esta; la; la; esas; esas.

Key Takeaways

And that's the end of Chapter 4! Here, you have learned:

- How to call every room in your house.
- How to call every object in your house.
- How to buy something in a store.

Chapter 5 is the last chapter of Book 2 and it will teach you everything about school, jobs and, most importantly, human relationships!

Chapter 5: School, Jobs and Relationships

El trabajo sin prisa es el mayor descanso para el organismo.
- Gregorio Marañón

At School

If you are a student, school is a very important part of your life. Therefore, no book would be complete without some school related vocabulary!

SPANISH	ENGLISH
la mochila	backpack
el lápiz	pencil
el bolígrafo	pen
la goma de borrar	eraser
la goma	rule
el maestro	teacher
el estudiante	student
la materia	subject
la clase	class
el examen	exam, test
las notas	grades
la universidad	university
la graduación	graduation
estudiar	to study
las clases particulares	private lessons
el aula	classroom
la tarea	homework
la beca	scholarship

Now, when we are in class, no matter the subject, there are some sentences we usually need to say. Let's check them out:

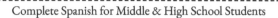

- *¿Podría repetir eso?* ("Could you repeat that?").
- *¿Podría hablar un poco más despacio?* ("Could you speak a bit more slowly?").
- *Perdón por llegar tarde* ("I'm sorry I'm late").
- *Tengo una pregunta* ("I have a question").
- *No entiendo* ("I don't understand").
- *¿Puede corregir mi trabajo?* ("Could you check my work?").
- *¿Podría deletrear eso?* ("Could you spell that?").
- *Necesito mejorar mis notas* ("I need to improve my grades").
- *Mis notas son buenas* ("My grades are good").
- *Aprobé el examen* ("I passed the test").
- *Reprobé el examen* ("I failed the test").

Remember that, when addressing your teacher, we usually use the formal Spanish "you", that is, usted, and its respective verb conjugations.

Relationships

Relationships are the backbone of human beings. Without them, we would be nothing!

SPANISH	ENGLISH
la familia	family
el amigo / la amiga	friend
la madre / la mamá	mother / mom
el padre / el papá	father / dad
los padres / los papás	parents
el hermano / la hermana	brother / sister
el abuelo / la abuela	grandfather / grandmother
el bisabuelo / la bisabuela	great grandfather / great grandmother
el tío / la tía	uncle / aunt
el primo / la prima	cousin
el novio / la novia	boyfriend / girlfriend
la pareja	partner
la cita	date
el mejor amigo / la mejor amiga	best friend
el esposo / la esposa	husband / wife
el padrastro / la madrastra	stepfather / stepmother
el hermanastro / la hermanastra	stepbrother / stepsister

| el cuñado / la cuñada | broher in law / sister in law |
| el suegro / la suegra | father in law / mother in law |

Social Media

And where do we, humans of the 21st century, conduct most of our social interactions? Well in social media, of course!

SPANISH	ENGLISH
el perfil	profile
la cuenta	account
la red social	social network
seguir	to follow
suscribir	to suscribe
compartir	to share
publicar	to publish
la contraseña	password
el usuario	user
el contenido	content
el video	video
la publicación	post
el mensaje privado	private message

Work Life

You might be a bit young yet, but, at some point, you'll have to join the work forces! If you want to be ready, study this vocabulary list!

SPANISH	ENGLISH
el trabajo	work
la oficina	office
tiempo parcial	half-time
tiempo completo	part-time
el / la pasante	intern

el jefe / la jefa	boss
el / la compañero/a de trabajo	coworker
renunciar	to quit
despedir	to fire
contratar	to hire
aplicar	to apply
entrenar	to train
ascender	to promote

Practice Time!

Read the text below and...

- Use one color to highlight family related vocabulary.
- Use another color to highlight social media related vocabulary.
- Use a third color to highlight work related vocabulary.

Mi mejor amiga Viviana y yo tenemos familias muy diferentes.

La familia de Viviana es enorme: tiene cuatro hermanos, tres tíos, cuatro tías y cerca de quince primos. Todos los años, en Navidad, se sacan una foto familiar y, cuando mi amiga me la muestra, siempre hay bebés nuevos... A Viviana le gusta tener una familia grande porque, en las reuniones familiares, los adultos siempre alquilan un castillo inflable para entretener a los niños. Además, siempre tiene a alguien con quien jugar o charlar.

Mi familia es muy diferente: solo somos mi papá, mi abuelo y yo. Sin embargo, a mí me gusta que sea una familia pequeña. Me llevo muy bien con mi papá y todavía mejor con mi abuelo, que es muy divertido y hasta juega videojuegos conmigo. ¡Ah! También está Toto, nuestro gato, que definitivamente es parte de la familia. Es como un hermano para mí... aunque un hermano un poco malhumorado. Pero los hermanos mayores de Viviana también son malhumorados.

Un dato curioso es que mi papá y uno de los tíos de Viviana se conocen de la secundaria y solían ser muy amigos. Se enteraron gracias a Instagram, viendo contactos en común. Lo gracioso es que mi papá solo tiene cuatro amigos en instagram: mi abuelo, yo, el tío de Viviana y... nuestro gato. Sí: Toto tiene un perfil de instagram. Se lo hice yo. Es que tengo muchas fotos lindas de él que me gusta compartir.

Algo que tenemos en común con Viviana es que, cuando seamos grandes, las dos queremos dedicarnos a las artes: yo quiero ser fotógrafa y Viviana quiere ser dibujante. Siempre decimos que trabajaremos juntas en nuestro propio estudio independiente.

Ⓐ Translation

My best friend Viviana and I have very different families.

Viviana's family is huge: she has four brothers, three uncles, four aunts, and about fifteen cousins. Every year at Christmas, they take a family photo, and when my friend shows it to me, I always notice new babies... Viviana likes having a big family because, during family gatherings, the adults always rent a bouncy castle to entertain the kids. Plus, she always has someone to play with or chat to.

My family is very different: it's just my dad, my grandfather, and me. However, I like that we are a small family. I get along very well with my dad and even better with my grandfather, who is a lot of fun and even plays video games with me. Oh! There's also Toto, our cat, who is definitely part of the family. He's like a brother to me... although a slightly grumpy one. But Viviana's older brothers are grumpy too.

A fun fact is that my dad and one of Viviana's uncles knew each other from high school and used to be great friends. They found out thanks to Instagram, by seeing mutual contacts. The funny thing is that my dad only has four friends on Instagram: my grandfather, me, Viviana's uncle, and... our cat. Yes, Toto has an Instagram profile. I created it for him. You see, I have many lovely photos of him that I like to share.

Something Viviana and I have in common is that, when we grow up, we both want to work in the arts: I'd like to be a photographer, and Viviana wants to be an artist. We always say that we'll work together in our own independent studio.

⊘ Answer Key

- Family related vocabulary: *familias, familia, hermanos, tíos, tías, primos, bebés, adultos, niños, papá, abuelo, hermano, hermanos mayores, tío.*
- Social media related vocabulary: *foto, videojuegos, Instagram, contactos en común, amigos en Instagram, perfil, compartir.*
- Work related vocabulary: *dedicarnos, fotógrafa, dibujante, trabajaremos, estudio independiente.*

Key Takeaways

Congratulations on your hard work! You have finished chapter 5, where you have learned:

- School related vocabulary and phrases.
- Social media related vocabulary and phrases.
- Basic work related vocabulary and phrases.
- Family related vocabulary.
- How to talk about your family or someone else's.

And just like that, you've reached the end of **Essential Spanish Vocabulary**! It's amazing all the vocabulary you have learnt! If you want to continue in this learning journey, move on to Book 3!

Conclusion

¡Felicidades!

You've reached the final chapter of this book, and your journey into the vibrant world of Spanish language and culture has been nothing short of remarkable. As we wrap up our exploration of basic Spanish vocabulary, it's essential to reflect on the immense significance of language and the invaluable role that a well-crafted journey plays in your learning adventure.

Vocabulary is the heartbeat of any language. Just as words and phrases are the building blocks of communication, they are also the keys that unlock doors to new experiences, connections, and opportunities. Whether you're a middle school or high school student, you've taken a crucial step towards becoming a confident Spanish speaker by delving into the vocabulary essentials covered in this book.

What sets **Essential Spanish Vocabulary** apart is its role as your trusty guide through this linguistic landscape. We've compressed diverse vocabulary topics into a single, user-friendly resource to simplify your learning experience. Whether you're looking for words for everyday life or for traveling, dining out, socializing, shopping, work, relationships or school, this book has equipped you with the essential tools to thrive in every one of those contexts.

As you finish this book, remember that your journey with Spanish doesn't end here. Language learning is a lifelong adventure, one filled with endless opportunities for growth and discovery. Continue to expand your vocabulary, practice your conversational skills, and immerse yourself in the rich tapestry of Spanish-speaking cultures.

Thank you for choosing **Essential Spanish Vocabulary**! May your newfound knowledge serve as a bridge to new friendships and exciting adventures!

Book 3

Spanish Short Stories for Young Beginners

Quick and Fun Stories to Learn Spanish Verbs, Conjugations And More!

Introduction

Embarking on the journey of learning Spanish tenses is like setting sail on a thrilling adventure, where each tense becomes a unique landmark along the way. If you've ever wondered how to express the past, present, or future in Spanish, you're in the right place. This book is your compass, guiding you through the intricacies of the Spanish verb conjugations and tense usage.

We understand that diving into the world of Spanish tenses may seem like a formidable task, especially for middle school and high school students. But fear not! With the right approach and a pinch of enthusiasm, you'll soon find yourself navigating the labyrinth of tenses with ease, becoming a natural Spanish speaker in no time.

In the pages that follow, we will embark on a voyage through four essential Spanish tenses:

- *Presente del Indicativo:* This tense allows us to talk about actions happening in the present. We also use it to express habits and convey general truths.
- *Pretérito Perfecto Simple:* Venture into the past with this tense as we uncover how to describe completed actions and events that occurred at specific moments.
- *Pretérito Imperfecto:* Explore the nuances of the past through this tense, perfect for narrating ongoing actions, setting scenes, or discussing past habits.
- *Futuro Imperfecto:* Peer into the future with this tense, as we learn to express future actions, intentions, and possibilities.

Mastering Spanish tenses can be challenging for English speakers. However, we want you to understand that challenges are opportunities in disguise.

Are you ready to embark on this adventure through the world of Spanish tenses? ¡Vamos!

First of all, you must bear in mind that, just like English, Spanish has both regular and irregular verbs. Sadly for new speakers, a lot of very common verbs (such as ser, tener and ir) are irregular. Bear in mind that the verb "to be" is also irregular in English. Fun fact: it's also irregular in several other languages, like French, Italian and Portuguese.

But we also have some very good news: most verbs are regular! Therefore, this book will focus on teaching you how to conjugate regular verbs. On the other hand, it will provide you with the irregular conjugation of some very common irregular verbs, which you'll have to learn by heart, as it's the only way!

We recommend that you rewrite irregular verbs and their conjugations in a piece of paper several times. This may seem pointless, but it's very useful for memorizing conjugations!

Having said that, you are ready for your first lesson.

Chapter 1: *Presente del indicativo*

> *En tres tiempos se divide la vida: en presente, pasado y futuro.*
> *De estos, el presente es brevísimo; el futuro, dudoso; el pasado, cierto.*
> - Lucio Anneo Séneca

When do we use it?

We use the *presente del indicativo* tense:
- For habits and routines: We use it to talk about things we do regularly. For example:
  Yo desayuno todas las mañanas ("I eat breakfast every morning").
- For facts or general truths: It's used to state facts or things that are generally true. For example:
  El sol sale por el este ("The sun rises from the east").

How do we conjugate regular verbs?

To conjugate regular verbs, we take the infinitive of the verb and we apply some changes. In Spanish, verbs in the infinitive always finish in one of these three endings: -ar, -er or -ir. The good thing is that, all the regular verbs ending in -ar change in the same way when we conjugate them in presente del indicativo. The same is true for all the regular verbs ending in -er and -ir. Each of these three endings determines the pattern which will be followed by the regular verbs.

First conjugation: verbs ending in *-ar*

Let's take a look at how a regular verb ending in *-ar* behaves when we conjugate in presente del indicativo. We'll start with the verb *hablar* ("to talk"):

PRONOUNS	VERBS
yo (I)	*habl**o***
tú (informal singular you)	*habl**as***
él / ella (he / she) *usted* (formal singular you)	*habl**a***
nosotros / nosotras (we)	*habl**amos***
ustedes (plural you) *ellos / ellas* (they)	*habl**an***

Here, *habl-* is what we call the root of the verb, which is the part that, in regular verbs, doesn't change.
So, if we want to conjugate a regular verb that ends in -ar in the present simple tense, all we have to do is add *-o*, *-as*, *-a*, *-amos* or *-an* to its root. Remember that, to obtain the root, we need to subtract the last two letters of the infinitive form: *-ar*, *-er* or *-ir*.

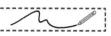

For example, for *cantar* ("to sing"), the root is *cant-*, and we conjugate it as follows:

PRONOUNS	VERBS
yo (I)	*canto*
tú (informal singular you)	*cantas*
él / ella (he / she) *usted* (formal singular you)	*canta*
nosotros / nosotras (we)	*cantamos*
ustedes (plural you) *ellos / ellas* (they)	*cantan*

Second conjugation: verbs ending in *-er*

Now, it's time to check the conjugation of regular verbs ending in *-er*, like *comer* ("to eat").

PRONOUNS	VERBS
yo (I)	*como*
tú (informal singular you)	*comes*
él / ella (he / she) *usted* (formal singular you)	*come*
nosotros / nosotras (we)	*comemos*
ustedes (plural you) *ellos / ellas* (they)	*comen*

Third conjugation: verbs ending in *-ir*

Finally, we can check the conjugation of regular verbs ending in *-ir*, like *partir* ("to leave").

PRONOUNS	VERBS
yo (I)	*parto*
tú (informal singular you)	*partes*
él / ella (he / she) *usted* (formal singular you)	*parte*
nosotros / nosotras (we)	*partimos*
ustedes (plural you) *ellos / ellas* (they)	*parten*

This one it's pretty similar to the pattern of *-er* verbs, right? To conjugate a regular verb that ends in *-ir* in the present simple tense, all we have to do is add *-o*, *-es*, *-e*, *-imos* or *-en* to its root.

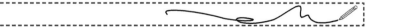

Irregular Verbs

In this section, we'll see the conjugation in *presente del indicativo* for of some of the most common irregular Spanish verbs:

Ser ("to be")

PRONOUNS	VERBS
yo (I)	*soy*
tú (informal singular you)	*eres*
él / ella (he / she) *usted* (formal singular you)	*es*
nosotros / nosotras (we)	*somos*
ustedes (plural you) *ellos / ellas* (they)	*son*

Tener ("to have")

PRONOUNS	VERBS
yo (I)	*tengo*
tú (informal singular you)	*tienes*
él / ella (he / she) *usted* (formal singular you)	*tiene*
nosotros / nosotras (we)	*tenemos*
ustedes (plural you) *ellos / ellas* (they)	*tienen*

Ir ("to go")

PRONOUNS	VERBS
yo (I)	*voy*
tú (informal singular you)	*vas*
él / ella (he / she) *usted* (formal singular you)	*va*
nosotros / nosotras (we)	*vamos*
ustedes (plural you) *ellos / ellas* (they)	*van*

Hacer ("to do")

PRONOUNS	VERBS
yo (I)	*hago*

tú (informal singular you)	*haces*
él / ella (he / she) *usted* (formal singular you)	*hace*
nosotros / nosotras (we)	*hacemos*
ustedes (plural you) *ellos / ellas* (they)	*hacen*

Practice Time!

Conjugate the following verbs in the present simple form:

Escribir ("to write")

PRONOUNS	VERBS
yo (I)	
tú (informal singular you)	
él / ella (he / she) *usted* (formal singular you)	
nosotros / nosotras (we)	
ustedes (plural you) *ellos / ellas* (they)	

Amar ("to love")

PRONOUNS	VERBS
yo (I)	
tú (informal singular you)	
él / ella (he / she) *usted* (formal singular you)	
nosotros / nosotras (we)	
ustedes (plural you) *ellos / ellas* (they)	

Nadar ("to swim")

PRONOUNS	VERBS
yo (I)	
tú (informal singular you)	
él / ella (he / she) *usted* (formal singular you)	
nosotros / nosotras (we)	

ustedes (plural you) *ellos / ellas* (they)	

Aprender ("to learn")

PRONOUNS	VERBS
yo (I)	
tú (informal singular you)	
él / ella (he / she) *usted* (formal singular you)	
nosotros / nosotras (we)	
ustedes (plural you) *ellos / ellas* (they)	

⊘ Answer Key

Escribir: escribo, escribes, escribe, escribimos, escriben
Amar: amo, amas, ama, amamos, aman
Nadar: nado, nadas, nada, nadamos, nadan
Aprender: aprendo, aprendes, aprende, aprendemos, aprenden

Story Time!

Read the following story:

En el bullicioso corazón de la Ciudad de Buenos Aires, vive una paloma llamada Tesla.

Por la mañana temprano, Tesla despierta al amanecer y se posa en la cornisa de un viejo edificio para recibir los primeros rayos de sol del día. Después, comienza su búsqueda de desayuno.

Tesla revolotea por las plazas y parques de la ciudad en busca de migajas y restos de pan dejados por los transeúntes. Se une a otras palomas en su búsqueda de alimento esparcido en el suelo. A veces, compite con los gorriones traviesos por las mejores migajas, pero siempre logra encontrar algo para saciar su apetito, especialmente si llega a tiempo para comer el maíz que una anciana llamada Doris reparte entre las aves todas las mañanas en Plaza Congreso.

Después del desayuno, Tesla disfruta de volar por la ciudad. Si hace calor, se baña en las fuentes de algún parque. Si hace frío o llueve, se refugia en los orificios de los rascacielos o los edificios antiguos.

Lo que menos le gusta a Tesla es cuando algún humano intenta patearla sin razón. Lo que más le gusta es cuando un humano le sonríe y le deja un pedacito de comida como un gesto de amabilidad.

Por la tarde, cuando el sol está en su punto más alto, Tesla se retira a la sombra de los árboles para descansar, mientras escucha el bullicio de la ciudad que nunca se detiene.

Al atardecer, cuando las luces de la ciudad comienzan a brillar, Tesla vuela hacia su nido en lo alto de un rascacielos. Allí, junto a su pareja, acurrucada y protegida, pasa la noche bajo el cielo de Buenos Aires.

Así vive Tesla su vida en el centro de la Ciudad de Buenos Aires, donde cada día es una nueva aventura en medio de la agitación urbana.

(A) Translation

In the bustling heart of Buenos Aires city, there lives a pigeon named Tesla.

Early in the morning, Tesla awakens at dawn and perches on the ledge of an old building to welcome the first rays of sunlight. Then, she begins her quest for breakfast.

Tesla flutters around the squares and parks of the city in search of crumbs and bits of bread left behind by passersby. She joins other pigeons in their quest for scattered food on the ground. Sometimes, she competes with mischievous sparrows for the best crumbs, but she always manages to find something to satisfy her appetite, especially if she arrives in time to eat the corn that an elderly woman named Doris distributes among the birds every morning in Plaza Congreso.

After breakfast, Tesla enjoys flying through the city. If the weather is warm, she bathes in the fountains of a park. If it's cold or rainy, she takes refuge in the nooks of skyscrapers or old buildings.

What Tesla likes the least is when a human tries to kick her for no reason. What she likes the most is when someone smiles at her and leaves her a little piece of food as an act of kindness.

In the afternoon, when the sun is at its highest point, Tesla retreats to the shade of the trees to rest, while listening to the never-ending buzz of the city.

At dusk, when the city lights begin to shine, Tesla flies to her nest at the top of a skyscraper. There, snuggled and protected alongside her partner, she spends the night under the Buenos Aires sky.

And so, Tesla lives her life in the heart of the City of Buenos Aires, where each day is a new adventure amidst the urban hustle and bustle.

💬 Glossary of Verbs

- *bañar:* to bathe
- *buscar:* to search
- *comenzar:* to begin
- *comer:* to eat
- *competir:* to compete
- *dejar:* to leave
- *disfrutar:* to enjoy
- *escuchar:* to listen
- *esparcir:* to scatter
- *gustar:* to like

- *intentar:* to try
- *llegar:* to arrive
- *lograr:* to manage
- *pasar:* to spend
- *posar:* to perch
- *recibir:* to receive
- *repartir:* to distribute
- *revolotear:* to flutter
- *saciar:* to satisfy
- *ser:* to be
- *sonreír:* to smile
- *unir:* to join
- *vivir:* to live
- *volar:* to fly

 ## Practice a Bit More!

1. Underline all the verbs of the story which are in the present tense.

2. Look them up in the glossary and classify them into regular and irregular verbs.

3. Fill in the blanks of the following sentences conjugating the verbs in brackets in the presente del indicativo tense:

a. Yo _____ (tener) dos hermanos.
b. Ella se _____ (llamar) Celeste.
c. Nosotros _____ (comer) tacos.
d. Mis amigos _____ (hablar) español.
e. Mi mamá _____ (amar) su trabajo.
f. Tú _____ (ser) mi mejor amigo.
g. Ustedes _____ (comprar) demasiados postres.
h. Yo _____ (ir) a la escuela a pie.
i. Mis padres y yo _____ (caminar) un poco todos los días.
j. Mis dos gatos _____ (beber) poca agua.

Answer Key

1. vive, despierta, se posa, recibir, comienza, revolotea, se une, compite, logra, llega, reparte, disfruta, hace, se baña, hace, se refugia, gusta, intenta, gusta, sonríe, deja, está, se retira, escucha, se detiene, comienzan, vuela, pasa, vive, es.

2. Look them up in the glossary and classify them into regular and irregular verbs.

Regular verbs:

- bañar: to bathe

- buscar: to search
- comer: to eat
- dejar: to leave
- disfrutar: to enjoy
- escuchar: to listen
- gustar: to like
- intentar: to try
- lograr: to manage
- posar: to perch
- pasar: to spend
- recibir: to receive
- repartir: to distribute
- revolotear: to flutter
- saciar: to satisfy
- unir: to join
- vivir: to live

Irregular verbs:

- comenzar: to begin
- competir: to compete
- esparcir: to scatter
- llegar: to arrive
- ser: to be
- sonreír: to smile
- volar: to fly

3.

a.   *Yo tengo dos hermanos.*
b.   *Ella se llama Celeste.*
c.   *Nosotros comemos tacos.*
d.   *Mis amigos hablan español.*
e.   *Mi mamá ama su trabajo.*
f.   *Tú eres mi mejor amigo.*
g.   *Ustedes compran demasiados postres.*
h.   *Yo voy a la escuela a pie.*
i.   *Mis padres y yo caminamos un poco todos los días.*
j.   *Mis dos gatos beben poca agua.*

Chapter 2: *Pretérito Perfecto Simple*

La memoria del corazón elimina los malos recuerdos y magnifica los buenos,
y gracias a ese artificio, logramos sobrellevar el pasado.
- Gabriel García Márquez

The *pretérito perfecto simple* tense is one of Spanish past tenses. It's used to talk about actions that happened in the past and are completed. We use it to describe what we did at a specific point in the past.

When do we use it?

We use the *pretérito perfecto simple* tense for:

• Finished past actions: We use it to talk about things that happened and finished in the past. For example: *Yo desayuné esta mañana* ("I ate breakfast this morning").

How do we conjugate regular verbs?

Just like in the *presente del indicativo* tense, we begin by checking whether the verb ends in *-ar*, *-er* or *-ir*.

First conjugation: verbs ending in *-ar*

Example: *Amar* ("to love")

PRONOUNS	VERBS
yo (I)	*am**o***
tú (informal singular you)	*am**as***
él / ella (he / she) *usted* (formal singular you)	*am**a***
nosotros / nosotras (we)	*am**amos***
ustedes (plural you) *ellos / ellas* (they)	*am**an***

Second and third conjugations: verbs ending in *-er* and *-ir*

For this tense, all regular verbs ending in *-er* and *-ir* follow the same pattern!

Example: *Escribir* ("to write")

PRONOUNS	VERBS
yo (I)	escrib**í**
tú (informal singular you)	escrib**iste**
él / ella (he / she) usted (formal singular you)	escrib**ió**
nosotros / nosotras (we)	escrib**imos**
ustedes (plural you) ellos / ellas (they)	escrib**ieron**

Irregular Verbs

Now we'll see the conjugation in *pretérito perfecto simple* for some of the most common irregular verbs in Spanish:

Ser ("to be")

PRONOUNS	VERBS
yo (I)	fui
tú (informal singular you)	fuiste
él / ella (he / she) usted (formal singular you)	fue
nosotros / nosotras (we)	fuimos
ustedes (plural you) ellos / ellas (they)	fueron

Tener ("to have")

PRONOUNS	VERBS
yo (I)	tuve
tú (informal singular you)	tuviste
él / ella (he / she) usted (formal singular you)	tuvo
nosotros / nosotras (we)	tuvimos
ustedes (plural you) ellos / ellas (they)	tuvieron

Ir ("to go"), which, in this tense, happens to be identical to the conjugation of *ser!*

PRONOUNS	VERBS
yo (I)	fui
tú (informal singular you)	fuiste

él / ella (he / she) *usted* (formal singular you)	*fue*
nosotros / nosotras (we)	*fuimos*
ustedes (plural you) *ellos / ellas* (they)	*fueron*

Estar ("to be")

PRONOUNS	VERBS
yo (I)	*estuve*
tú (informal singular you)	*estuviste*
él / ella (he / she) *usted* (formal singular you)	*estuvo*
nosotros / nosotras (we)	*estuvimos*
ustedes (plural you) *ellos / ellas* (they)	*estuvieron*

Practice Time!

Conjugate the following verbs in the *pretérito perfecto simple* tense:

Bailar ("to dance")

PRONOUNS	VERBS
yo (I)	
tú (informal singular you)	
él / ella (he / she) *usted* (formal singular you)	
nosotros / nosotras (we)	
ustedes (plural you) *ellos / ellas* (they)	

Caminar ("to walk")

PRONOUNS	VERBS
yo (I)	
tú (informal singular you)	
él / ella (he / she) *usted* (formal singular you)	
nosotros / nosotras (we)	
ustedes (plural you) *ellos / ellas* (they)	

Correr ("to run")

PRONOUNS	VERBS
yo (I)	
tú (informal singular you)	
él / ella (he / she) *usted* (formal singular you)	
nosotros / nosotras (we)	
ustedes (plural you) *ellos / ellas* (they)	

⊘ Answer Key

Bailar: bailé, bailaste, bailó, bailamos, bailaron
Caminar: caminé, caminaste, caminó, caminamos, caminaron
Correr: corrí, corriste, corrió, corrimos, corrieron

Story Time!

Read the following story:

Luca entró a su apartamento con la bolsa de las compras y se sorprendió al encontrar a su novia, Laura, que vivía allí con él, sentada en el suelo llorando.

——¿Qué pasó? ——se asustó el joven, dejando la bolsa a un lado y arrodillándose junto a ella——. ¿Estás bien?

Laura negó con la cabeza.

——Me despidieron ——confesó, secándose las lágrimas.

Luca se sintió increíblemente sorprendido: Laura era la persona más responsable que conocía. Siempre había sido muy estudiosa en la universidad y, aunque su sueño era ser una bióloga famosa, trabajaba muy duro en un laboratorio para pagar sus estudios de posgrado.

——¿Cómo pueden despedirte? ——quiso saber Luca——. ¿A ti? ¿Qué pasó?

——Solo sugerí una pequeña alternativa para que nuestro trabajo fuera más ecológico. Me dijeron que mis intereses no iban alineados a los de la compañía.

——¿Te despidieron por eso? ¡Qué tontería!

——De verdad que no es justo ——estuvo de acuerdo su novia——. Siento que me he esforzado muchísimo toda mi vida, pero no soy buena en ningún trabajo. Ni en el restaurante, ni aquí... ¿Acaso soy una inútil que no sirve para nada más que estudiar?

——¡Claro que no, Laura! ——se indignó Luca——. ¿Cómo puedes decir eso? Además, en el restaurante no te despidieron.

——Pero no era buena.

——¿Qué importa si no eras buena mesera?

——Una persona responsable debe ser buena en todo.

——Nadie es bueno en todo ——sonrió Luca——. Escucha, no es tan grave. Solo debemos buscarte otro trabajo, uno en donde tu jefe no ame la contaminación.

Finalmente, Laura se rió un poco y Luca también. Estaba a punto de sugerirle a su novia que hicieran algo divertido para olvidar aquel fiasco, cuando el celular de ella comenzó a sonar.

——Es Analía ——anunció Laura, mirando su pantalla. Analía era una compañera de trabajo——, pero no quiero hablar con ella. Toma: contesta tú.

Luca tomó el teléfono y respondió a la llamada:

——Hola, Analía.

——¡Hola, Luca! ¿Por qué contestas tú? ¿Dónde está Laura?

——Está en la ducha ——mintió el joven——. ¿Quieres que le deje un mensaje?

——Pues sí: pregúntale si mañana puede comprar ella el café antes de venir al laboratorio.

Luca titubeó, confundido:

——¿Qué quieres decir? ——dudó.

——Mañana es mi turno, pero debo llevar a mi perro al veterinario, así que quería saber si Laura podía hacerlo en mi lugar.

——Pero... ¿No la despidieron?

——¿De qué estás hablando? ——se extrañó Analía——. Laura no fue despedida... La regañaron un poco, pero nada más.

——Laura... Analía está diciendo que no te despidieron.

——Todavía ——aclaró Laura——, pero mi jefe estaba muy enfadado. ¿Acaso no sabes lo que eso significa? ¡Van a despedirme en cualquier momento!

Luca no podía creer lo exagerada que era su novia: como nunca cometía errores, si alguien la regañaba

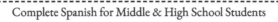

una sola vez, creía que el mundo se había terminado. Estaba demasiado sorprendido como para hacer otra cosa que no fuera volver a llevar el teléfono a su oreja y hablar con Analía:

——De acuerdo. Le diré lo del café.

(A) Translation

Luca entered his apartment with the grocery bag and was surprised to find his girlfriend, Laura, who lived with him, sitting on the floor crying.

"What happened?" said the startled young man, leaving the bag aside and kneeling next to her. "Are you okay?"

Laura shook her head.

"I got fired," she confessed, wiping away her tears.

Luca felt incredibly surprised. Laura was the most responsible person he knew. She had always been a diligent student in college, and even though her dream was to become a famous biologist, she worked very hard in a lab to pay for her graduate studies.

"How can they fire you?" Luca wanted to know. "What happened?"

"I just suggested a small alternative to make our work more environmentally friendly. They told me my interests didn't align with the company's."

"They fired you for that? That's ridiculous!"

"It really isn't fair," her girlfriend agreed. "I feel like I've worked so hard my whole life, but I'm not good at any job. Not at the restaurant, not here... Am I just useless, only good for studying?"

"Of course not, Laura!" said Luca indignantly. "How can you say that? Besides, you weren't fired from the restaurant."

"But I wasn't good at it."

"What does it matter if you weren't a good waitress?"

"A responsible person should be good at everything."

"No one is good at everything," said Luca, smiling. "Listen, it's not that bad. We just have to find you another job where your boss doesn't love pollution."

Finally, Laura laughed a little, and Luca did too. He was about to suggest they do something fun to forget about that fiasco when her phone started ringing.

"It's Analía," Laura announced, looking at her screen. Analía was a coworker. "But I don't want to talk to her. Here, answer for me."

Luca took the phone and answered the call.

"Hello, Analía."

"Hi, Luca! Why are you answering? Where's Laura?"

"She's in the shower," lied the young man. "Do you want me to leave her a message?"

"Well, yes. Ask her if she can buy some coffee tomorrow before coming to the lab."Luca hesitated, confused.

"What do you mean?" he asked.

"Tomorrow is my turn, but I have to take my dog to the vet, so I wanted to know if Laura could do it for me."

"But... Didn't she get fired?"

"What are you talking about?" Analía was puzzled. "Laura wasn't fired... She was scolded a little, but that was it."

"Laura... Analía says you weren't fired."

"Not yet," Laura clarified, "but my boss was very angry. Don't you know what that means? They're going to fire me any moment now!"

Luca couldn't believe how exaggerated his girlfriend was. Since she never made mistakes, if someone scolded her even once, she thought the world had ended. He was too surprised to do anything else but return the phone to his ear and talk to Analía.

"Okay. I'll tell her about the coffee."

💬 Glossary of Verbs

- *aclarar:* to clarify
- *arrodillarse:* to kneel
- *asustarse:* to be startled
- *confesar:* to confess
- *decir:* to say
- *dejar:* to leave
- *estar:* to be
- *extrañarse:* to be puzzled
- *importar:* to matter

- *indignarse:* to be indignant
- *negar:* to deny
- *pasar:* to happen
- *querer:* to want
- *reír:* to laugh
- *secar:* to dry
- *sentir:* to feel
- *sugerir:* to suggest
- *tener:* to have
- *titubear:* to hesitate

Practice a Bit More!

1. Underline all the verbs of the story which are in *pretérito perfecto simple*.

2. Fill in the blanks of the following text conjugating the verbs in brackets in *pretérito perfecto simple* or *presente del indicativo*.

Normalmente, yo _____ (cenar) en casa, pero ayer _____ (ir) a un restaurante y _____ (pedir) pizza. _____ (estar) deliciosa. Francamente, ese lugar _____ (ser) un muy buen restaurante.

⊘ Answer Key

1. *entró, se sorprendió, pasó, asustó, negó, despidieron, confesó, se sintió, quiso, pasó, sugerí, dijeron, despidieron, estuvo, se indignó, despidieron, sonrió, se rió, comenzó, anunció, tomó, respondió, mintió, titubeó, dudó, despidieron, regañaron, despidieron, aclaró, podía.*

2. *Normalmente, yo ceno en casa, pero ayer fui a un restaurante y pedí pizza. Estuvo deliciosa. Francamente, ese lugar es un muy buen restaurante.*

Chapter 3: *Pretérito Imperfecto*

En lo pasado está la historia del futuro.
- Juan Donoso Cortés

The *pretérito imperfecto* tense is the other past tense we'll discuss in this book. This tense is used to describe past actions that were ongoing or in progress when another action took place. We also use it to talk about past habits and to set the stage for a past event.

When do we use it?

We use the pretérito imperfecto tense for:

- Ongoing actions in the past: We use it to talk about actions that were happening in the past without a specific endpoint. For example:
  Yo desayunaba cuando sonó el teléfono ("I was eating breakfast when the phone rang").
- Descriptions and background information: It's used to provide descriptions, set the scene, or give background information about past events. For example:
  El sol brillaba y los pájaros cantaban ("The sun was shining and the birds were singing").

How do we conjugate regular verbs?

As always, we begin by checking whether the verb ends in *-ar*, *-er* or *-ir*.

First conjugation: verbs ending in *-ar*

Example: *Amar* ("to love")

PRONOUNS	VERBS
yo (I)	*ama**ba***
tú (informal singular you)	*ama**bas***
él / ella (he / she) *usted* (formal singular you)	*ama**ba***
nosotros / nosotras (we)	*am**ábamos***
ustedes (plural you) *ellos / ellas* (they)	*ama**ban***

Second and third conjugations: verbs ending in *-er* and *-ir*

For this tense, all regular verbs ending in *-er* and *-ir* follow the same pattern!

Example: *Escribir* ("to write")

PRONOUNS	VERBS
yo (I)	*escrib**ía***
tú (informal singular you)	*escrib**ías***
él / ella (he / she) *usted* (formal singular you)	*escrib**ía***
nosotros / nosotras (we)	*escrib**íamos***
ustedes (plural you) *ellos / ellas* (they)	*escrib**ían***

Irregular Verbs

Now it's time to check the conjugation in *pretérito imperfecto* for some common irregular verbs:

Ser ("to be")

PRONOUNS	VERBS
yo (I)	*era*
tú (informal singular you)	*eras*
él / ella (he / she) *usted* (formal singular you)	*era*
nosotros / nosotras (we)	*éramos*
ustedes (plural you) *ellos / ellas* (they)	*eran*

Ir ("to go")

PRONOUNS	VERBS
yo (I)	*iba*
tú (informal singular you)	*ibas*
él / ella (he / she) *usted* (formal singular you)	*iban*
nosotros / nosotras (we)	*íbamos*
ustedes (plural you) *ellos / ellas* (they)	*iban*

Practice Time!

Conjugate the following verbs in the *pretérito imperfecto* tense:

Pintar ("to paint")

PRONOUNS	VERBS
yo (I)	
tú (informal singular you)	
él / ella (he / she) *usted* (formal singular you)	
nosotros / nosotras (we)	
ustedes (plural you) *ellos / ellas* (they)	

Beber ("to drink")

PRONOUNS	VERBS
yo (I)	
tú (informal singular you)	
él / ella (he / she) *usted* (formal singular you)	
nosotros / nosotras (we)	
ustedes (plural you) *ellos / ellas* (they)	

Jugar ("to play")

PRONOUNS	VERBS
yo (I)	
tú (informal singular you)	
él / ella (he / she) *usted* (formal singular you)	
nosotros / nosotras (we)	
ustedes (plural you) *ellos / ellas* (they)	

⊘ Answer Key

Pintar: pintaba, pintabas, pintaba, pintábamos, pintaban
Beber: bebía, bebías, bebía, bebíamos, bebían
Jugar: jugaba, jugabas, jugaba, jugábamos, jugaba

Story Time!

Read the following story:

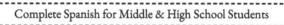
Agustín amaba los juegos de rol.

Cada tres semanas, él y sus amigos se reunían en casa de su vecina Celeste y pasaban al menos cinco horas jugando. A Agustín le encantaban estos juegos porque le permitían sumergirse en un mundo de fantasía en donde podía ser cualquier cosa.

Sin embargo, su madre no estaba de acuerdo:

——Antes de esos juegos, estudiabas mucho más ——se quejó una tarde——. Te quitan demasiado tiempo.

Agustín le respondió que eso no era verdad, pues sus amigos y él solo jugaban una vez cada tres semanas.

——Sí, pero pasas mucho tiempo planeando esas campañas e inventando personajes ——insistió su ¡madre——. Antes dedicabas ese tiempo a estudiar.

——¿Pero qué esperas? ¿Que el pobre viva solo para estudiar? ——lo defendió su padre——. Déjalo tener su pasatiempo. No hace daño a nadie.

——No entiendo por qué no puede tener un pasatiempo normal ——dijo enfadada la madre——, como tocar un instrumento o practicar deporte.

——¿Y crees que eso es normal? ——rió el padre——. Los niños de hoy se lo pasan jugando videojuegos o haciendo desastres... Al menos él usa su imaginación. Además, ¿no recuerdas lo que hacías tú cuando tenías su edad?

Agustín observó que su madre se ponía nerviosa.

——No sé de qué hablas. Por cierto, creo que oí el timbre.

Luego de decir eso, se marchó de la cocina, en donde tenía lugar la conversación. Agustín aprovechó ese momento para acercarse a su papá.

——¿De qué hablabas? ——quiso saber——. ¿Qué hacía mamá cuando tenía mi edad?

Su padre se rió y le respondió en un susurro:

——No te enteraste por mí, pero tu madre dedicó su adolescencia a escribir fanfiction. Incluso ganó un concurso cuando tenía catorce años. Así que dile eso la próxima vez que no quiera dejarte jugar.

Ⓐ Translation

Agustín loved role-playing games.

Every three weeks, he and his friends would gather at their neighbor Celeste's house and spend at least five hours playing. Agustín loved these games because they allowed him to immerse himself in a

fantasy world where he could be anything.

However, his mother didn't agree:

"Before these games, you used to study much more," she complained one afternoon. "They take up too much of your time."

Agustín replied that it wasn't true, as he and his friends only played once every three weeks.

"Yes, but you spend a lot of time planning those campaigns and creating characters," his mother insisted. "You used to dedicate that time to studying."

"But what do you expect? That the poor boy lives only to study?" his father defended him. "Let him have his hobby. It's harmless."

"I don't understand why he can't have a normal hobby," said his mother, angry. "Like playing a musical instrument or practicing sports."

"And do you think that's normal?" his father laughed. "Kids today spend their time playing video games or causing trouble... At least he's using his imagination. Besides, don't you remember what you did when you were his age?"

Agustín noticed his mother getting nervous.

"I don't know what you're talking about. By the way, I think I heard the doorbell."

After saying this, she left the kitchen, where the conversation was taking place. Agustín took that moment to approach his dad.

"What were you talking about?" he wanted to know. "What did Mom do when she was my age?" His father laughed and whispered in response:

"You didn't hear it from me, but your mother spent her teenage years writing fanfiction. She even won a contest when she was fourteen. So tell her that next time she doesn't want to let you play."

Glossary of Verbs

- *amar:* to love
- *defender:* to defend
- *dedicar:* to dedicate
- *encantar:* to delight
- *enfadarse:* to get angry
- *esperar:* to expect
- *ganar:* to win
- *hacer:* to do/make
- *insistir:* to insist

- *observar:* to observe
- *pasar:* to spend
- *permitir:* to allow
- *practicar:* to practice
- *quejarse:* to complain
- *recordar:* to remember
- *reunirse:* to gather/meet
- *ser:* to be
- *tener:* to have
- *tocar:* to play
- *usar:* to use

 Practice a Bit More!

1. Underline all the verbs of the story which are in *pretérito imperfecto*.

2. Fill in the blanks of the following text conjugating the verbs in brackets either in *pretérito perfecto* simple or *pretérito imperfecto*.

Ese día, Luisa _____ (salir) temprano de su casa y descubrió que _____ (llover) a cántaros. _____ (odiar) la lluvia y no _____ (querer) mojarse, así que _____ (tener) que regresar al apartamento para buscar su paraguas.
De nuevo en la calle, _____ (caminar) hacia la estación de autobús haciendo lo posible por no mojarse, pero, debido al viento, _____ (ser) difícil.
Por fin _____ (llegar) el autobús, pero _____ (estar) demasiado lleno, así que Luisa _____ (decidir) esperar al siguiente.
Cuando _____ (llegar) el segundo autobús, se subió y, tras tomar asiento, _____ (sacar) su celular para ver si _____ (tener) mensajes de sus amigos.
En efecto, _____ (haber) un mensaje.
_____ (ser) de su amiga Carla, diciéndole que ese día no habría clases por la fuerte tormenta.

✓ Translation

That day, Luisa left her house early and discovered that it was pouring. She hated the rain and didn't want to get wet, so she had to go back to her apartment to get her umbrella.
Back on the street, she walked towards the bus station trying her best not to get wet, but due to the wind, it was difficult.
Finally, the bus arrived, but it was too crowded, so Luisa decided to wait for the next one.
When the second bus arrived, she got on and, after taking a seat, took out her cellphone to see if she had any messages from her friends.
Sure enough, there was a message.
It was from her friend Carla, telling her that there would be no classes that day due to the heavy storm.

✓ Answer Key

1. amaba, se reunían, pasaban, encantaban, permitían, podía, estaba, estudiabas, era, jugaban, dedicabas, hacías, tenía, hablabas, hacía, tenía catorce años.

2. Ese día, Luisa salió temprano de su casa y descubrió que llovía a cántaros. Odiaba la lluvia y no quería mojarse, así que tuvo que regresar al apartamento para buscar su paraguas.
    De nuevo en la calle, caminó hacia la estación de autobús haciendo lo posible por no mojarse, pero, debido al viento, era difícil.
    Por fin llegó el autobús, pero estaba demasiado lleno, así que Luisa decidió esperar al siguiente.
    Cuando llegó el segundo autobús, se subió y, tras tomar asiento, sacó su celular para ver si tenía mensajes de sus amigos.
    En efecto, había un mensaje.
    Era de su amiga Carla, diciéndole que ese día no habría clases por la fuerte tormenta.

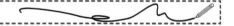

Chapter 4: *Futuro Imperfecto*

Deberíamos tratar de ser los padres de nuestro futuro en lugar de los descendientes de nuestro pasado.
- Miguel de Unamuno

The *futuro imperfecto* tense in Spanish is used to describe actions that will take place in the future.

When do we use it?

We use the futuro imperfecto tense to:

- Talk about the future with time markers like *mañana* ("tomorrow"), *el año que viene* ("next year"), etc. For example:
  El mes que viene visitaré a mi padres ("Next month I will visit mi parents").
- Make predictions. For example:
  Hoy será un buen día ("Today is going to be a good day").

How do we conjugate regular verbs?

Lucky for you, it's very simple to conjugate verbs in this tense!

As long as the verb is regular, all you have to do is take the infinitive form of the verb and add the following endings, according to who the subject is:

PRONOUNS	VERBS
yo (I)	*é*
tú (informal singular you)	*ás*
él / ella (he / she) *usted* (formal singular you)	*á*
nosotros / nosotras (we)	*emos*
ustedes (plural you) *ellos / ellas* (they)	*án*

Let's check an example.

Example: *Escribir* ("to write")

PRONOUNS	VERBS
yo (I)	escribir**é**
tú (informal singular you)	escribir**ás**
él / ella (he / she) *usted* (formal singular you)	escribir**á**
nosotros / nosotras (we)	escribir**emos**
ustedes (plural you) *ellos / ellas* (they)	escribir**án**

Irregular Verbs

There are also some irregular verbs, of course. Let's check a few:

Tener ("to have")

PRONOUNS	VERBS
yo (I)	tendré
tú (informal singular you)	tendrás
él / ella (he / she) *usted* (formal singular you)	tendrá
nosotros / nosotras (we)	tendremos
ustedes (plural you) *ellos / ellas* (they)	tendrán

Hacer ("to do")

PRONOUNS	VERBS
yo (I)	haré
tú (informal singular you)	harás
él / ella (he / she) *usted* (formal singular you)	hará
nosotros / nosotras (we)	haremos
ustedes (plural you) *ellos / ellas* (they)	harán

Practice Time!

Conjugate the following verbs in the *futuro imperfecto* tense:

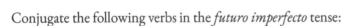

Comer ("to eat")

PRONOUNS	VERBS
yo (I)	
tú (informal singular you)	
él / ella (he / she) *usted* (formal singular you)	
nosotros / nosotras (we)	
ustedes (plural you) *ellos / ellas* (they)	

Soñar ("to dream")

PRONOUNS	VERBS
yo (I)	
tú (informal singular you)	
él / ella (he / she) *usted* (formal singular you)	
nosotros / nosotras (we)	
ustedes (plural you) *ellos / ellas* (they)	

Hablar ("to talk")

PRONOUNS	VERBS
yo (I)	
tú (informal singular you)	
él / ella (he / she) *usted* (formal singular you)	
nosotros / nosotras (we)	
ustedes (plural you) *ellos / ellas* (they)	

⊘ Answer Key

Comer: pintaré, pintarás, pintará, pintaremos, pintarán
Soñar: soñaré, soñarás, soñará, soñaremos, soñarán
Hablar: hablaré, hablarás, hablará, hablaremos, hablarán

Story Time!

Read the following story and conjugate the verbs in brackets in the *futuro simple* form:

Mi hermano Leandro siempre está hablando de su futuro. Dice que _____ (ser) un streamer famoso y que _____ (vivir) en una enorme mansión, donde _____ (criar) muchos perros que _____ (adoptar) de la calle.

Además, dice que _____ (viajar) por el mundo y _____ (conocer) todos los países de sus sueños, como Egipto, Japón, Costa Rica y Australia. Y, cuando le pregunto cómo planea entender a la gente, responde que _____ (aprender) a hablar al menos diez idiomas distintos.

Personalmente, creo que mi hermano es poco realista. Yo también sé lo que quiero ser al crecer, pero al menos no hablo de eso todo el tiempo. Además, mis sueños son más razonables: me _____ (convertir) en el hombre más rico del mundo vendiendo las letras de mis canciones y _____ (usar) el dinero para abrir mi propio parque temático.

✓ Answer Key

será, vivirá, criará, adoptará, viajará, conocerá, aprenderá, convertiré, usaré.

✎ Read a Bit More!

Read the following text:

Yo creo que, en el futuro, las ciudades serán muy diferentes a lo que conocemos hoy en día. Serán lugares donde la tecnología estará en todas partes, pero también donde la naturaleza tendrá un papel fundamental en la vida cotidiana.

En esta visión del futuro, las calles estarán repletas de vehículos eléctricos y autónomos que se desplazarán silenciosamente por la ciudad. El aire estará limpio y fresco, gracias a la amplia adopción de energías limpias y renovables. Las casas serán inteligentes, capaces de ajustar automáticamente la temperatura y la iluminación según las preferencias de sus habitantes.

Pero lo más sorprendente será la conexión entre la tecnología y la naturaleza. Los edificios estarán cubiertos de jardines verticales y terrazas verdes, creando oasis de vegetación en medio de la jungla de concreto. Las calles tendrán árboles y arbustos que proporcionarán sombra y oxígeno fresco. La energía se generará a partir de paneles solares y turbinas eólicas integradas en la infraestructura urbana.

En esta ciudad del futuro, la educación será accesible para todos a través de plataformas en línea de alta calidad. Las personas podrán aprender y desarrollar sus habilidades desde cualquier lugar y en cualquier momento. La igualdad de oportunidades será una realidad, ya que la tecnología eliminará las barreras geográficas y económicas.

La salud también experimentará avances significativos. Los dispositivos médicos conectados y los sistemas de telemedicina permitirán un monitoreo constante de la salud, brindando diagnósticos tempranos y tratamientos personalizados. La prevención será clave, con un enfoque en la alimentación saludable y el ejercicio.

En este futuro, la sociedad valorará más la sostenibilidad y la conservación del medio ambiente. La conciencia ambiental será parte integral de la cultura, y las personas se esforzarán por vivir de manera más ecológica y responsable. Además, la carne será producida en los laboratorios, así que no existirá la violencia contra los animales.

En resumen, yo creo que, en el futuro, nuestras ciudades serán lugares donde la tecnología y la naturaleza coexistirán en armonía. Será un mundo de posibilidades ilimitadas, donde la calidad de vida y el cuidado del planeta serán prioridades fundamentales.

💬 Glossary of Verbs

- *desplazar:* to move
- *ajustar:* to adjust
- *crear:* to create
- *cubrir:* to cover
- *proporcionar:* to provide
- *generar:* to generate
- *aprender:* to learn
- *desarrollar:* to develop
- *eliminar:* to eliminate
- *brindar:* to offer
- *valorar:* to value
- *esforzarse:* to strive

✍️ Practice a Bit More!

1. Underline all the verbs of the text which are in *futuro imperfecto*.

2. Complete the following sentences with your predictions for the future:

En el futuro, las ciudades... _____

En las ciudades del futuro, nosotros... _____

En el futuro, yo... _____

✓ Answer Key

1. *serán, serán, estará, tendrá, estarán, desplazarán, estará, serán, será, estarán, tendrán, proporcionarán, generará, será, podrán, será, eliminará, experimentará, permitirán, será, valorará, será, se esforzarán, será, existirá, serán, coexistirán, será, serán.*

Conclusion

Congratulations! You have completed a remarkable journey through the intricate world of Spanish tenses. Your dedication, perseverance, and curiosity have brought you to this point, and we couldn't be prouder of your accomplishments.

Mastering Spanish tenses is no small feat, especially for middle school and high school students. Yet, you've shown that, with the right guidance and determination, you can conquer the challenges and become a more confident and proficient Spanish speaker. Your efforts have unlocked the doors to effective communication, storytelling, and a deeper understanding of Spanish-speaking cultures.

As you finish this book, we'd like to offer some final words of encouragement and guidance on how to continue improving your Spanish skills:

Remember that practice makes perfect: The more you use the tenses in real-life situations, the more they become second nature. Engage in conversations with native speakers, join language exchange programs, watch TV shows with subtitles on, or find online forums where you can practice.

Use websites such as https://www.spanishconjugation.net/ to learn how to conjugate new irregular verbs!

Read and listen: Dive into Spanish literature, newspapers, magazines, videos and podcasts. These resources expose you to diverse vocabulary and provide insights into Hispanis culture and society.

Use language learning apps: There are numerous language learning apps and websites designed to help you practice and enhance your skills. Incorporate them into your daily routine.

Watch films and TV shows in Spanish: Watching Spanish-language movies and TV series is an enjoyable way to improve your listening skills and familiarize yourself with colloquial expressions. Another thing you can do is watch a movie or TV show that you have watched several times in English, but this time do it in Spanish!

Seek feedback: Don't be afraid to ask for feedback from native speakers or teachers. Constructive criticism can help you identify areas for improvement.

Travel and immerse: If the opportunity arises, visit Spanish-speaking countries. Immersion in the culture and daily life is one of the most effective ways to improve your language skills.
You've shown incredible dedication by completing this book, and we have no doubt that your passion for learning will lead you to even greater heights in your Spanish language journey. *¡Mucho éxito!*

Made in United States
Troutdale, OR
09/30/2024